Hurricane IIB Combat Log

No. 151 Wing RAF

North Russia 1941

Hugh Harkins

Hurricane IIB Combat Log

© Hugh Harkins 2013

Published by Centurion Publishing
Glasgow
United Kingdom
G65 9YE

ISBN 10: 1-903630-46-0
ISBN 13: 978-1-903630-46-4

This volume first published in 2013

The Publishers and Author would like to thank all organizations and services for their assistance and contributions in the preparation of this publication

CONTENTS

INTRODUCTION

No.151 Wing RAF (Royal Air Force) was formed at the end of July 1941 as a two Squadron Hurricane wing incorporating No.'s 81 and 134 Squadrons, which were formed in the last days of July 1941 at RAF Leconfield.

The formation of the Wing followed discussions at the highest level of British government following the German invasion of the Soviet Union in June 1941. Operation Barbarossa had met with enormous success, the Soviet Forces being defeat in pitched battles, falling back all along the front. Britain was under pressure to aid its new ally, the Soviet Union. Although unwilling to provide the asked for ground forces, the British government decided that all possible material aid should be given to the Soviet Union to keep her in the fight. British Prime Minister Churchill was under no illusions; knowing well that Britain alone was never going to be able to provide the huge armies necessary to defeat Germany. The Soviet Union was now a way for the Germans to be fought en-mass.

As well as material aid, it was decided to provide a RAF Wing to fight alongside the Red Air Force, while at the same time instructing Soviet pilots on the Hawker Hurricane IIB fighters so that they would form a nucleus of combat pilots from which a large force of Soviet Flown Hurricanes Squadrons would be spawned.

FORMATION OF NO.151 WING RAF & PREPARATIONS FOR OPERATIONS IN RUSSIA

In the weeks following the German invasion of the Soviet Union, Great Britain, under great pressure from its old enemy turned new ally, looked at a number of options for rendering assistance to the Soviets, who were reeling from the German onslaught. While the Soviets were asking for assistance to the tune of perhaps 30 British Army Divisions with supporting air units, the British government was unwilling to commit ground forces to the theatre. However, it endeavoured to render all material assistance it could, from its own stocks and from lend lease items being brought over from the United States. The decision to supply the Soviets with Hawker Hurricane fighters was followed by a high level decision to send a RAF Hurricane Wing to conduct operations alongside the Soviet Air Force. The Murmansk front was selected, not least because it was the easiest theatre to reach from the United Kingdom. The aircraft and supplies, along with Squadron and wing personnel and infrastructure could be shipped around the North Cape beyond Norway and into the Kola Peninsula.

During July 1941, plans were set in motion for the formation of No.151 Wing RAF, which would administer 2 Squadron; No's 81 and 134, which were to be formed at RAF Leconfield from a nucleus of pilots transferred from other fighter Squadrons.

Formation of No.81 Squadron

On 29 July 1941, No.81 Squadron commenced formation at RAF Leconfield, York's. Under the command of Squadron Leader A.H. Rook, a small element of the Squadron had actually arrived from Fairwood Common, South Wales the day before. This nucleus of what would become 81 Squadron consisted of the

Commanding Officer, the Squadron Adjutant and nine pilots, "the entire personnel of 'A' Flight, No.504 Squadron under Flight Sergeant O'Malley". This nucleus of pilots consisted of F/Sgt's Haw, Reed, Smith, Waud and Anson and F/Lt Rook, P/O's McGregor, Bush and Holmes, P/O Conybeare, Adjutant and F/O Kennedy, the Intelligence Officer who joined the unit at Leconfield.

Throughout the last few days of July and the first 12 days of August, the formation of the Squadron was completed and additional pilots had joined the Squadron "with F/Sgt. Barkus as disciplinary Flight Sergeant and Flight Sergeant Baker in charge of 'B' Flight". The other new pilots consisted of P/O's. Walker Ramsey, both of whom arrived from No.402 Squadron; P/O Edisto from No.123 Squadron, and Sergeant Pilots Rigby and Crewe allocated from No.605 Squadron, Mulroy and Carter allocated from No.615 Squadron and Bishop and Sims who came from No.43 Squadron.

The Squadron personnel departed RAF Leconfield for Liverpool in the early morning of the 12th to be embarked on the steamer ss. *Llanstepan Castle* for the voyage to North Russia. The Squadron CO (Commanding Officer) and 11 Pilots remained as they were due to embark on HMS *Argus* with the Squadrons Hurricane IIB fighters. F/Lt. Rook had previously departed on another ship with a small Squadron advance party.

Formation of No.134 Squadron

Copy of Headquarters Fighter Command Movement Order
Signal 0.89 Dated 27/7/41.

Pilots and personnel of 1 flight of 17 Squadron to consist of 9 operational pilots and ground personnel of 1 flight plus the Squadron Leader and Adjutant to move to Leconfield by P.M. 28th July, 1941, to form nucleus 134 Squadron coming under 151 Wing to proceed overseas at short notice. Pilots to take full flying clothing. Servicing echelon not to move. Aircraft not to move.

No.134 Squadron was officially formed at Leconfield on 31 July 1941. The establishment at this time consisted of 102 ground personnel and the following pilots.

S/Ldr. A.G. Miller Commanding Officer
F/O. S.R. Palmer Adjutant
F/O. W.L. Blackbourn Intelligence Officer

"A" Flight	"B" Flight
F/Lt. V.W. Berg	F/Lt. J.R. Ross
P/O. Elkington	P/O. N. Cameron
P/O M.E. Sheldon	P/O. K.M. Wollaston
P/O. R.H. Furneaux	F/Sgt Barnes L.J.
Sgt. Clarke S.Mc	F/Sgt. McCann T.A.
Sgt. Campbell B.J.	Sgt. Griffiths R
Sgt. Gould A.J.	Sgt. Fry S.R.
Sgt. Kirvan R.P.F.	Sgt Knapton P
Sgt. Kiel H	Sgt. Douglas J.C.I.

On 12 August 1941, the 134 Squadron Adjutant, F/O. Palmer, the Intelligence Officer, F/O Blackbourn, P/O, Wollaston and six of the Sgt. Pilots departed Leconfield bound for Liverpool. Similar elements of No.81 Squadron, along with some No. 151 Wing personnel also departed for Liverpool, all being embarked on the ss *Llanstephan Castle* at 09.00 hours.

As well as the personnel of 81 and 134 Squadrons the 151 Personnel were also embarked on the *LLanstephan Castle*, including the Wing Commander, G.R. Isherwood, A.F.C and his staff.

The *Llanstephan* Castle sailed at 1500 hours on 12 August 1941, the ship arriving at Scapa Flow on the 15th, sailing again on the 17th, bound for Iceland, where it arrived on the 20th, departing Iceland on the 21st, bound for North Russia, the coast of which was reached on 30 August. The ship moved into Archangel Sound, near Archangel on 31 August to take on a pilot, who berthed the ship in Archangel on 1 September 1941. Once berthed, Air Vive Marshall Collier, the Head of Air Section, British Military Mission to Moscow, came aboard, along with Group Captain Bird.

On 1 September F/O. Kennedy and Flight Sergeant 'Discipline' 134 Squadron were flown in a "Douglas" to Vayenga; the planned operating base for 151 RAF. The following day, F/O. Conybeare and a Corporal from the "Orderly Room" arrived at Vayenga on a Consolidated Catalina Flying Boat.

The following day "The adjutant, N.C.O. 1/c Orderly Room, Discip. N.C.O. and two airmen, included in party of 36, comprising Wing Signals Sitting party,

Wing Assistant Adjt. Intelligence Officer and Adjt. 81 Squadron and 27 Airmen, proceeded by river steamer to Archangel Aerodrome with a view to travelling by air to Murmansk".

"Only Intelligence Officer and 7 airmen were able to proceed in Douglas passenger plane. Balance of party were not authorized to travel, apparently owing to lack of fighter escort at Murmansk for 2 Catalina Flying Boats in which they were intended to travel".

On the 3rd, the Catalina Flying Boats were allowed to proceed, "with 14 in each party", taking off from Archangel aerodrome at 13.00 hours for Vayenga, near Murmansk, where they arrived at 18.30 hours. It is thought that the aircraft may have been attacked during the flights, the 134 Squadron records noting "During this flight two aircraft approached and believed to have opened fire (16.00 hours), a detour was made and route resumed".

Over the course of the next few days the Wing and Squadrons personnel made various ways to Vayenga aerodrome. After disembarking from the ss *Llanstephan Castle*, some were transferred to a Russian Hospital Ship, which took them to Kandalaksha, where they embarked on a train, which transported them to Vayenga, where they arrived on 6 September. The Wing Commander and his Wing party, along with personnel of 81 and 134 Squadrons had arrived at Murmansk, Vayenga on two Destroyers on the 5th. Another party, after disembarking from the *Llanstephan Castle*, was embarked on the destroyer HMS *Electra*, which took them to Murmansk, from where they moved to nearby Vayenga.

All told the Wing and Squadron personnel numbered in the region of 300, which were housed in "brick barrack blocks". On the 4th, before many of the Wing and Squadrons personnel had arrived at Vayenga, a "slight air raid" could be heard a few miles from the airfield.

The Commanding Officer of 81 & 134 Squadrons and the remaining pilots had departed RAF Leconfield on a Handley Page Harrow at 12.30 hours on 16 August 1941, arriving at RAF Abbotsinch at 14.45; departing here by road at 09.45 the following morning, bound for Port Greenock where the embarked on the aircraft carrier HMS *Argus* at 11.45 am. HMS *Argus*, along with a troopship, the ss *Empress of Canada* and a Destroyer escort (later RAF Bristol Blenheim aircraft joined the escort), departed Port Greenock at 01.00 hours on 19 August. HMS *Argus* arrived at Scapa Flow in the Orkney Islands, anchoring at 03.00 on the morning of 20 August. She sailed from Scapa at 07.00 on 30 August, bound for the launch point for the Wings Hurricanes to take off for their destination in North Russia.

During the final stages of the aircraft carriers voyage to the launch point, the ship encountered the fogs and sea mists, which were a feature of these northern climes.

HMS *Argus* was equipped with two Grumman Martlet fighters for air defense during the passage North, these eventually being transferred to the carrier HMS *Victorious*, which was planning an air attack on Petsamo, North Finland.

On the 7th of September, the C/O of 81 Squadron and the 11 other pilots took off from HMS *Argus* and landed their Hurricane IIB's at Vayenga. These 12 Hurricanes were armed with only six machine guns per aircraft in order to save weight; a necessary expedient if the aircraft were to be successfully launched from the *Argus*.

No.134 Squadron Hurricanes lifted off HMS *Argus* starting at 07.00 on the morning of 7 September 1941. During the take off's two of the Squadrons Hurricanes struck a "ramp at end of Flight Deck, damaging under-carriage". The consequences of this would be felt when the aircraft arrived at their destination. The protective wooden platting over the accelerator had been installed when the carrier had been employed operating Queen Bee aircraft. The platting had remained, and proved a hazard to fighter operations, eventually being removed when the carrier was at Gibraltar some time later.

Those on the deck of the *Argus* feared the worst as one of the Hurricanes sank down and disappeared beyond the ships bows, reappearing again a few seconds later as the aircraft struggled to gain height.

The Squadron report stated the possible causes of the aircraft striking the ramp were outlined as the following:

     (1) Still air (Carrier travelling at approx. 20 knots).
     (2) Short take-off deck giving only 400' run.
     (3) Existence of ramp. (Understood to be used for Queen Bee Aircraft).

The 12 Hurricanes of 134 Squadron were Z5205 flown by S/Ldr. Miller, Z3763 flown by F/Lt. Ross, Z5206 flown by F/Lt. Berg, Z5159 flown by P/O. Elkington, Z5253 flown by P/O. Furneaux, BD823 flown by Sgt. Campbell, Z5120 flown by F/Sgt. Barnes, Z2978 flown by P/O. Cameron, Z4013 flown by P/O. Sheldon, BD699 flown by Sgt. Clarke, Z5134 flown by Sgt. Gould, and Z5210 flown by F/Sgt. McCann.

The Hurricanes flew over the sea, making land fall some 70 miles to the East of the Kola Inlet, arriving at Vayenga aerodrome between 08.15 and 08.30 hours after around 1 hour 15 minutes in the air.

Hurricane Z5206, which had struck the ramp on taking off from HMS *Argus*, crash landed at Vayenga, due to damage to the undercarriage. The pilot, F/Lt. Berg was not injured, but the aircraft was declared u/s. Both undercarriage legs of Hurricane BD823, flown by Sgt. Campbell, collapsed during the landing and the aircraft nosedived into the ground. This aircraft, which like Z5206, had damaged its undercarriage during the take off from HMS *Argus*, was declared u/s.

The Hurricanes of 134 Squadron were dispersed "around the North West perimeter of the Drome, in semi-sunken butts, with camouflaged cover, three quarters overall, camouflaged with natural material, which is very effective".

As the Squadrons settled in, the C/O's of 81 and 134 Squadrons attended a conference with the Wing Commander and Soviet Admiral Kuznetsov, the Air Officer Commanding Local Group and Soviet Forces in the Kola Peninsula.

There was a serious shortage of maintenance materials and tooling, reducing the amount of work that could be carried out on the aircraft. On the 8th another conference was held between the Wing Commander, the Squadron Commanders and the Soviet Group Commander, with a similar conference held on the 9th. On this date there was an air raid in the local area, with some aircraft passing over the aerodrome.

A pair of Russian Destroyers arrived at Murmansk, from Archangel, carrying Browning machine guns, ammunition and spares for the Wing. However, it was discovered that there was a lack of "rear sear release units, also fire and safe units; guns were fitted with Mark 1 blast tube adaptor and therefore unsuitable for use in the Hurricane Mark II aircraft". This meant that the Wings Hurricanes (planning called for both squadrons of 151 Wing to be equipped with 19 Hurricanes each) would not be able to be armed with their full complement of 12 x 0.303 in machine guns. This deficiency would plague the Wing throughout the next six weeks of operations, with many aircraft reduced to six working guns, although some were able to operate with eight, some with ten and a few would eventually be equipped with a full complement of twelve guns. No.134 Squadron was able to salvage the guns from the two aircraft that crashed on the 7th, distributing these among the remaining aircraft to make eight serviceable guns in each aircraft. Many 81 Squadron aircraft had to operate with only six guns.

There was no flying reported for the 10th; the Wing Commander and Squadron Commanders having another daily conference as the Wing was prepared for operations. The situation in the area was extremely serious; a recent offensive placing the Germans only some 25-30 miles from Murmansk.

Soviet soldiers work on excavating the dispersal area for the newly arrived
Hurricanes of 151 Wing RAF at Vayenga aerodrome, some 12 miles from the
City of Murmansk on Russia's Northern Coast. In the background, a Hurricane
IIB from No.134 Squadron is undergoing servicing. *RAF*

This Soviet Military Map shows the operational areas of the Squadrons of 151 Wing operating from Vayenga aerodrome near Murnansk, Russia. The Wing came under control of Admiral, Kuznetzov, Commander of Allied forces in the Kola Peninsula.

Previous page top: A Hawker Hurricane IIB flies low over Vayenga aerodrome near Murmansk during a beat up watched by personnel of No.151 Wing, with Hurricanes at dispersal. RAF

Previous page bottom: A three aircraft section of No.81 Squadron Hurricane IIB's flies over another 81 Squadron Hurricane, Z3768 FK 49 at its waterlogged dispersal on Vayenga aerodrome. RAF

Above: The Headquarters building of No.151 Wing, RAF, near Vayenga Field, with RAF sentries on guard. RAF

2

NO.81 SQUADRON OPERATIONS - SEPTEMBER AND OCTOBER 1941

By the 11 September, eight of No. 81 Squadrons Hurricanes were equipped with six x 0.303 in machine guns in workable condition. This allowed the Squadron to commence operational patrols with a "sector recco" planned for that afternoon.

11.9.1941: 4 No.81 Squadron Hurricane IIB's took off at 15.05 hours on a Sector Recco under command of S/Ldr. Rook flying aircraft BD792, F/Sgt. Haw flying Z4018, P/O. Ramsey flying Z5157 and F/O. McGregor flying Z3746. This patrol proved uneventful and the four aircraft landed back Vayenga at 16.05 hours.

At least four other Hurricane flights were recorded on this date: P/O. Bush (un-recorded aircraft number), Sgt. Anson flying Z5207, Sgt. Reed flying Z4006 and Sgt. Waud fling Z5227. These sorties, which lasted 1 hour, 10 minutes, were recorded as "Sector Reco's", but were actually gun testing sorties

12.9.1941: A 3 aircraft patrol was launched at 11.20 hours; Sgt. Smith flying Z3746, P/O. Walker flying Z5157 and S/Ldr. Rook flying BD792. This patrol landed at 1210 hours.

At 11.45 hours, one Hurricane, Z4018, flown by F/Sgt. Haw, was launched on an interception, landing at 12.30.

Apparently the same aircraft and pilot were again launched on an interception at 1455, along with Sgt. Smith flying Z3746 and P/O. Walker flying Z5157. This flight encountered six enemy aircraft and in the ensuing combat F/Sgt. Haw claimed one Me.109E (Confirmed) and P/O. Walker claimed one Me.109 (confirmed). On the debit side Hurricane Z3746 was shot down, Sgt. Smith being killed. His aircraft was apparently struck by at least one cannon shell and he subsequently crash landed, but was killed in the crash. Squadron Form 541 states 2 Me.109's were shot down, however, Form 540 claims' that three were shot down. Form 540 goes on to state that "P/O Bush attacked a Me.110 in the morning, hits being observed in the belly". However, Form 541 initially shows no record of this, nor does it initially record P/O. Bush as having flown an operational sortie on this date. However, a supplement at the end of Form 541 shows the record of P/O. Bush's flight and records the claim of the damaged Me.110

The Form 540 goes on to state "Three Me.109E's were shot down in the afternoon by P/O. Walker, F/Sgt. Haw of "A" Flight and Sergeant Pilot Waud of "B" Flight. It is assumed that this is an additional reference to the above combats. Form 541 initially shows no sortie flown by Sergeant Pilot Waud on this date, but a supplement at the end of the form shows Sgt. Waud flying in Hurricane IIB Z4006. Form 540 continues "In addition Sgt. Pilot Waud attacked and damaged a Henschel 126 which was being covered by 6 Me.109E". The Supplement to Form 541 records 1 Me.109 confirmed shot down and 1 Henschel 126 damaged and then changed to confirmed destroyed by Sgt. Waud. On 26 September 1941, the Russian Observer Corp confirmed that the Henschel 126 thought to have been damaged was in fact destroyed. The supplement to Form 541 goes on to record the patrol flights of Sgt. Rigby and P/O. Edmiston, both of which were initially omitted from the initial Form 541 record.

The following Narrative of the 12 September combats comes from the 81 Squadron Operation Report:

"The patrol took off at 1505 hours and intercepted at 1525 hours, height 3,500 feet. Flight Sergeant Haw, Red (patrol) leader put a ten second beam burst into the enemy aircraft leader which crashed in flames. P/O. Walker, Red 2 then attacked an Me.109 which was on Red Leaders tail, giving it two bursts of a few seconds each after which it crashed in flames. Sgt. Waud, Blue Leader, put two bursts into the Henschel from which smoke poured. He then broke away owing to Me.109's being close, attacking one of them at ground level. This enemy aircraft then crashed in flames after the third attack."

Squadron pilot strength was increased when F/Lt. Rook arrived from Archangel with Sergeant Pilots Bishop and Carter. The following day Sergeant Sims arrived at the airfield from Archangel and Sergeant Smith, whom had been killed in action the previous day, was buried.

13

Before the freezing wintry conditions of the latter part of the Wings Russian operations, the Hurricanes operated in rudimentary conditions plagued by wet weather, flooded ground and mud. Previous page top: This Tropicalised Hurricane IIB, Z3977 FN-55 is being serviced at Vayenga in September 1941. Previous page bottom: 81 Squadron ground crew attach a trolley-accumulator cable to one of the Squadrons Hurricanes at Vayenga. Above: 81 Squadron Hurricane IIB, Z3977 FN-55, at readiness. RAF

PERSONAL   COMBAT REPORT

Sector Serial No……………………….............(A)   **Not given.**
Serial No. of Order detailing Flight or Squadron to
    Patrol……………………………………(B)   **"   "**
Date…………………………………………..(C)   **12th September 1941.**
Flight, Squadron…………………………….....(D)   **Flight: A   Sqdn 81.**
Number of Enemy Aircraft…………………...(E)   **One.**
Type of Enemy Aircraft……………………..(F)   **Me.109 E.**
Time Attack was Delivered………………….(G)   **1530 hrs.**
Place Attack was Delivered…………………..(H)   **Over Enemy Lines**
                                                        West of Murmansk.
Height of Enemy…………………………....(J)   **4000 ft.**
Enemy Casualties……………………………..(K)   **One Me.109 E. Des**
Our Casualties…………Aircraft……………(L)
                          Personnel…………(M)
GENERAL REPORT………………………..(R)   **I took off at 1505 hrs.**
as Red 2 While flying on patrol at 3500 ft. sighted 5 109's and one Hs.126.
Followed Red 1 into attack at about 1522 hrs. Broke away and engaged
one ('one' is scored out and replaced with handwritten 'two') **two of the 109's**
concurrently in head on attack. When about 500 ft. saw the a/c Red 1 was
attacking go past me breaking into flames and heading straight for the
ground. Climbed up and saw a 109 on Red 1's tail, headed in and gave the
a/c a couple of bursts of a few seconds each.

The 109 broke away and fell towards ground pouring out smoke.
Followed him down and saw him roll over – then regain upright position
he then burst into flames and crashed. Returned to base with Red 1,
landed at 1550 hrs.

                           Signature……………….**P/O.**
                           Section   **Red**
               OC   Flight   **"A"**
                           Squadron   Squadron No. **81.**
                           Signature of S/Ldr.

RAF Form1151

Form "F"

PERSONAL   COMBAT REPORT

Sector Serial No...(A)	Not given.
Serial No. of Order detailing Flight or Squadron to Patrol..(B)	" "
Date...(C)	12. 9. 41.
Flight, Squadron..(D)	Hurricane II. Flight: "B" Sqdn 81.
Number of Enemy Aircraft.......................(E)	One.
Type of Enemy Aircraft...........................(F)	Me.110.
Time Attack was Delivered.......................(G)	
Place Attack was Delivered......................(H)	Over Enemy Lines N.W. of Murmansk.
Height of Enemy......................................(J)	
Enemy Casualties....................................(K)	One Me.110 (E)?
Our Casualties............Aircraft................(L)	Nil.
Personnel.............(M)	Nil.

GENERAL REPORT.............................(R)   At 1145 a.m. I was ordered to patrol Zone 2 with Blue Section 81 Squadron and when I was about 20 miles N.W. of Murmansk I sighted a plane coming head on towards me at the same height. When about 300 yards away it evidently recognised me and turned over to starboard showing me a yellow belly and wings with black crosses and the twin tails on a Me.110. I, as Blue 1 got in a two second burst and hits were observed by myself and Blue 11 in the body of the machine. E.A. then dived straight down to 100 ft. and made due west for home. I chased it over trees and round hills swapping shots with the rear gunner but it gradually drew away and I left it when it got too far out of range.

Signature...................P/O.
Section   **Blue**
OC   Flight   **"B"**
Squadron   Squadron No. **81.**
Signature of S/Ldr.

RAF Form1151

Form "F"

PERSONAL   COMBAT REPORT

Sector Serial No...(A) **Not given.**
Serial No. of Order detailing Flight or Squadron to
    Patrol...(B) **"   "**
Date...(C) **12th September 1941.**
Flight, Squadron.......................................(D) **Hurricane   II**
(hand written)
Flight: A Sqdn 81.
Number of Enemy Aircraft.......................(E) **One.**
Type of Enemy Aircraft............................(F) **Me.109 E.**
Time Attack was Delivered.......................(G) **1525 hrs.**
Place Attack was Delivered.......................(H) **Over Enemy Lines**
West of Murmansk.
Height of Enemy.....................................(J) **4000 ft.**
Enemy Casualties.....................................(K) **One Me.109 E. Des**
Our Casualties.............Aircraft................(L)
               Personnel.............(M)
GENERAL REPORT.............................(R) **At 1525 hrs. on 12.9.41.**
**whilst leading a patrol of five Hurricanes over the enemy lines I
intercepted five Me.109 E's escorting a Hs.126. My height was 3500 ft.
The e/a were approaching from ahead and slightly to the left, and as I
turned towards them, they turned slowly to their right. I attacked the
leader as he turned and gave him a ten second burst from the full beam
position. The e/a rolled on to its back, and as it went down burst into
flames. I did not see it crash owing to taking evasive action, but Red 2
confirms that it passed him in a 70 degree dive at 500 ft., smoke and
flames still pouring from it.**

Signature..................F/Sgt.
Section **Red**
OC   Flight **"A"**
Squadron   Squadron No. **81.**
Signature of S/Ldr.

RAF Form1151

Form "F"

PERSONAL   COMBAT REPORT

Sector Serial No...(A)	**Not given.**
Serial No. of Order detailing Flight or Squadron to Patrol..(B)	**" "**
Date..(C)	**12th September 1941.**
Flight, Squadron......................................(D)	**Hurricane II** (hand written) **Flight: B Sqdn 81.**
Number of Enemy Aircraft..........................(E)	**Two.**
Type of Enemy Aircraft..............................(F)	**Henschel 126 & Me.109.**
Time Attack was Delivered..........................(G)	**1525 Hrs.**
Place Attack was Delivered.........................(H)	**Over Enemy Lines W. of Murmansk.**
Height of Enemy.......................................(J)	**4000 ft.**
Enemy Casualties......................................(K)	**Hs.126 Probable And Me.109 Des**
Our Casualties............Aircraft................(L)	
Personnel.............(M)	

GENERAL REPORT...............................(R)   **At the time when the above action took place I was leader of Blue Section. I found myself in a favourable position to attack the Hs.126, and after my delivering a short burst from the beam it turned and dived away steeply westwards. I followed, overtaking rapidly and fired a burst at** ('very close' scored out and replaced by '50 ft'. hand written) **range. As I passed over the top of the e/a a thick cloud of white smoke poured from it. This was observed by Blue 2 (Sgt. Rigby) I did not see what happened to the Henschel, as I broke away and climbed again to 4000 ft. and had to look out for Messerschmitts, and take violent weaving action.**

From my height I saw a Me.109 and a Hurricane going round in a circle at ground level. I dived, and using my advantage of speed and height, was enabled to deliver a rear quarter attack, followed by afport (should probably read 'a port') **qtr-attack. I then got on the tail of the e/a and again closed to** ('very close' scored out and replaced with '50 ft.' hand written) **range and passed over the top of the e/a. As I delivered my last attack I saw smoke coming from the e/a/, which was flying very low and just after I passed over it, I saw it crash in flames. I did not see the other Hurricane again and presumably it was Sgt. Smith, who was missing from the engagement.**

	Signature...............**Sgt Pilot.**
	Section **Blue Section**
OC	Flight **"B" Flight**
	Squadron Squadron No. **81.**
	Signature of S/Ldr.

RAF Form1151

13.9.1941: Three Hurricanes took off on patrol at 14.50 hours followed by a fourth at 14.55. These aircraft, BD792 flown by S/Ldr. Rook, Z4018 flown by F/O. McGregor, Z5157 flown by P/O. Ramsey and Z5209 flown by P/O. Walker, landed at 16.05 hours. A supplement to Form 541 shows two additional flights, Z5207 flown by Sgt. Rigby and Z5122 Flown by F/Lt. Rook; these flights lasting 1 hour ten minutes and probably being part of the same group that took off between 14.50 and 14.55.

14.9.1941: S/Ldr. Rook in BD792, F/Sgt. Haw in Z4018, Sgt. Waud in Z5157 and Sgt. Carter in Z5029 took off at 12.05 hours for local flying, landing back at 12.45. Later S/Ldr. Rook in BD792 and the new pilot, Sgt. Sims in Z4018, took off on a local flying training flight at 18.30 hours, landing back at 19.10. The supplement to From 541 shows three other Hurricane Flights by P/O. Edmiston flying Z5227, F/Lt. Rook flying BD697 and P/O. Bush flying Z4006, these sorties lasting 1 hour 5 minutes.

15.9.1941: At 11.10 hours 4 Hurricanes, BD792 flown by S/Ldr. Rook, Z5209 flown by P/O. Walker, Z4018 flown by F/Sgt. Haw and BD822 flown by F/O. McGregor, took off on an attempted interception of German aircraft, landing back at 12.15.

At 11.40 hours 4 Hurricanes, BD792/flown by Ldr. Rook, BD822 flown by Sgt. Waud, Z5157 flown by P/O. Ramsey and Z5209 flown by Sgt. Sims, took off on an attempted interception, landing back at 15.45. At 18.20 hours 4 Hurricanes, BD792 flown by S/Ldr. Rook, Z5208 flown by F/Sgt. Haw, Z5209 flown by P/O. Walker and Z5228 flown by F/O. McGregor, took off on an attempted interception, landing back at 19.10.

Additional recorded in a Form 541 supplement, consist of the following listed as "Patrols", but more likely non-operational local training flights. Z5227 (Sgt. Reed), 1 hour, 10 mins., BD697 (F/Lt. Rook), 1 hour, 5 mins., Z4017 (Sgt. Anson), 1 hour, 10 mins., BD697 (F/Lt. Rook), 1 hour, Z4017 (P/O. Edmiston), 1 hour, Z5227 (Sgt. Bishop), 1 hour, Z5207 (Sgt. Anson), 1 hour, BD697 (F/Lt. Rook), 50 mins., Z4017 (Sgt. Anson), 55 mins., Z5207 (P/O. Edmiston), 50 mins. and Z4006 (Sgt. Reed), 50 mins.

17.9.1941: At 0910 hours S/Ldr. Rook took off in Hurricanc IIB BD792 to test the aircrafts guns, landing back at 0930.

At 1830 hours, S/Ldr. Rook flying BD792, Sgt. Sims flying Z5228, Sgt. Waud flying BD822 and F/Sgt. Haw flying Z5208, took off on an interception. Form 540 initially shows only this four aircraft flight, however, Form 541 states that eight Hurricanes, "four from each flight" were involved, taking off at "1830 hours to cover the withdrawal of Russian bombers. The Combat Reports for this date clearly indicate that both 'A' and 'B' Flights were involved. A supplement at the end of Form 541 shows the additional sorties being P/O. Bush flying Z4017, Sgt. Rigby flying Z3977, P/O. Edmiston flying Z5227 and Sgt. Anson flying Z5207, all taking off at 18.35 on a defensive patrol.

The Hurricane formations intercepted a formation of 8 Me.109's, which were themselves preparing to attack the formation of Russian bombers. The C/O, S/Ldr. Rook, launched a "quarter stern" attack on an Me.109E, firing a two second burst, claiming to have hit the German aircraft on the radiator. He continued after the Me.109 in a chase lasting some five minutes, during which he claimed to have slowed it to around 150 miles per hour, using up all his ammunition in the process. The damaged 109 was then attacked by two other Hurricanes, Red 2, Sgt. Sims and Green 1, Sgt. Anson, after which it "crashed in flames". Following this, Green I came under attack from four Russian fighters, but took evasive action to shake them off. In his Combat Report S/Ldr. Rook cites Red 2 and Black 1 not Green 1 as conducting the attack on the 109.

A Me.109E was attacked by Yellow Leader, F/Sgt. Haw, who conducted a stern attack with no "visible effect". Yellow Leader then conducted a quarter attack, firing a three second burst at a range of 150 yards, the enemy aircraft catching fire, followed by the pilot bailing out.

Blue Leader, P/O. Bush, engaged a Me.109, out turning it to enable a "two second starboard burst" at the enemy aircraft, which was then on fire. A further burst of machine gun fire resulted in the enemy aircraft crashing.

A sideline to the battle was the fact that a German Me.110 was also shot down, although it was unclear if anyone form 81 Squadron had engaged it let alone hit it. The aircraft was confirmed shot down by the Russian Observer Corp., who credited to 81 Squadron. It is more probable, however, that the 110 was brought down by the Russian fighters, which were in the area.

Ground crew moves 81 Squadron Hurricanes from their hides for servicing in September 1941. RAF

Form "F"

PERSONAL   COMBAT REPORT

Sector Serial No.................................(A)	**Not given.**
Serial No. of Order detailing Flight or Squadron to Patrol.................................(B)	**" "**
Date.................................(C)	**17· 9. 41.**
Flight, Squadron.................................(D)	**Hurricane II.**
	Flight: "B" Sqdn 81.
Number of Enemy Aircraft.................................(E)	**One.**
Type of Enemy Aircraft.................................(F)	**One Me.109.E.**
Time Attack was Delivered.................................(G)	**19.15 hrs.**
Place Attack was Delivered.................................(H)	**Nr. Balncha;**
	N.W. of Murmansk.
Height of Enemy.................................(J)	**4000 ft.**
Enemy Casualties.................................(K)	**One Me.109. E.**
Our Casualties............Aircraft...............(L)	**Nil.**
Personnel............(M)	

GENERAL REPORT.................................(R)   **On 17.9.41. as leader
of Green section 81 Squadron, I took off from base at 18.30 hrs. to cover
the withdrawal of Russian bombers. My section was weaving, and at
approx. 19.15 hrs. I saw two Me.109.E.'s approach from the starboard at
9000 ft. The E.A. immediately dived, the Squadron following them I
stayed above the Squadron and continued to weave until I was able to
intercept an E.A. then some 5000 ft. below. I dived on it, and a Hurricane
which was then attacking broke away. The Me.109 continued to take
gentle evasive action. I made a port quarter attack developing to astern. I
fired five bursts from 150 yds. At the conclusion of which the E.A. caught
fire underneath the engine, and dived, the hood and several pieces flew
off. The E.A. then crashed in flames beside a lake.
I observed another fight to starboard and turned to investigate, but a
concentrated attack by four Russian fighters caused me to take evasive
action. I then returned to base, rejoining the remainder of the Squadron
on the circuit.**

Signature.................**P/O.**

Section **Green**

OC   Flight   **"B"**

Squadron   Squadron No. **81.**

Signature of S/Ldr.

RAF Form1151

Form "F"

PERSONAL   COMBAT REPORT

Sector Serial No...(A)	**Not given.**
Serial No. of Order detailing Flight or Squadron to Patrol..(B)	" "
Date..(C)	**17· 9. 41.**
Flight, Squadron..(D)	**Hurricane II.** **Flight: "A" Sqdn 81.**
Number of Enemy Aircraft........................(E)	**8**
Type of Enemy Aircraft............................(F)	**One Me.109.E.**
Time Attack was Delivered.......................(G)	**18.55 hrs.**
Place Attack was Delivered.......................(H)	**Over enemy lines, West. of Murmansk.**
Height of Enemy.......................................(J)	**8000 ft.**
Enemy Casualties......................................(K)	**1 Me.109.E. Destroyed**
Our Casualties............Aircraft................(L)	**Nil.**
Personnel.............(M)	

GENERAL REPORT..............................(R)   **At the time of the above action I was leader of Yellow Section. Two Me.109.E's dived over and passed in front of us. I attacked the second E.A. as he turned and dived Westwards. I made an astern attack at about 200 yds, range firng a three secs. Burst, with no visible effect. The E.A. then turned to the right across me, and I delivered a quarter attack from about 150 yds. Firing another burst of three seconds. During this attack smoke began to pour from the E.A. a large piece flew off him, and he rolled onto his back, and went into a vertical dive. An enemy pilot who bailed out was identified by the Russian Observer Corps. As being the pilot of the machine which I attacked. The piece of E.A. which flew off was probably the hood being jettisoned.**

Signature..................F.Sgt. 754259. (Haw)
Section **Yellow.**
OC Flight   **"A"**
Squadron   Squadron No.
Signature of S/Ldr.

RAF Form1151

Form "F"

PERSONAL   COMBAT REPORT

Sector Serial No.......................................(A)
Serial No. of Order detailing Flight or Squadron to
      Patrol..(B)
Date..(C)   17. 9. 41.
Flight, Squadron..............................(D)   Hurricane II.
                                                              Flight: "B" Sqdn 81.
Number of Enemy Aircraft.......................(E)   One.
Type of Enemy Aircraft..........................(F)   One Me.109.E.
Time Attack was Delivered.......................(G)   19.15 hrs.
Place Attack was Delivered......................(H)   Nr. Balncha;
                                                              N.W. of Murmansk.
Height of Enemy.................................(J)   5000 ft.
Enemy Casualties................................(K)   One Me.109. E.
Our Casualties.............Aircraft...............(L)   Nil.
                          Personnel............(M)   Nil.
GENERAL REPORT...........................(R)   On date mentioned I
was leading "B" Flight 81 Squadron after being ordered up at 18.30 hrs. to
cover retreat of some Russian Bombers. At 19.15 hrs. two Me.109.E's were
sighted about to attack the bombers. On looking behind I noticed 6 more
Me.109's diving from above and behind and turned sharply to port to
engage the outside 109 which was nearest. A dog fight ensued in which I
was able to out-turn the E.A. and deliver a 2 sec. burst from the starboard
quarter. Thick black smoke came from E.A. as it dived to earth, and
getting in another short burst E.A. burst into flames and crashed into hill.
A second E.A. was diving upon me as I looked behind but after turning
sharply to port, I lost E.A. and after cruising round for another 5 mins. I
returned to base.

                              Signature..................P/O. (Bush)
                                   Section **Blue**
                              OC   Flight   **"B"**
                                      Squadron   Squadron No. **81.**
                                      Signature of S/Ldr.

RAF Form1151

                                                   Form "F"

PERSONAL   COMBAT REPORT

Sector Serial No..(A)   Not given.

Serial No. of Order detailing Flight or Squadron to
    Patrol...(B)   "   "

Date...(C)   17· 9. 41.

Flight, Squadron.................................(D)   Hurricane II.
                                            Flight: "A" Sqdn 81.

Number of Enemy Aircraft......................(E)   8

Type of Enemy Aircraft...........................(F)   Me.109.E.

Time Attack was Delivered......................(G)   1855.

Place Attack was Delivered......................(H)   Over Enemy Lines
                                            West. of Murmansk.

Height of Enemy.....................................(J)   8000 ft.

Enemy Casualties...................................(K)   One   Me.109
                          Destroyed

Our Casualties............Aircraft................(L)   Nil.
                        Personnel.............(M)

GENERAL REPORT.............................(R)   I was leading 8 A/C, 4
from each flight. Two 109E's dived over us and passed in front. I attacked
the leader and delivered a quarter stern attack at 150 yds, Burst 2 secs. hit
radiators, glycol poured out and covered my front screen, chased for
about 5 mins. And pumped all my bullets into same, slowed it up and left
it to Red 2 and Black 1. Saw 109.E. crash by side of lake on fire.

                               Signature..................S/Ldr. (Rook)

                                     Section   Red

                            OC   Flight   "A"

                                     Squadron   Squadron No. 81.

In general melee one Me.110. was credited by Russian Observers to the
Squadron.

                           Signature of S/Ldr.

RAF Form1151   O.C 81. Squadron.

Form "F"

PERSONAL   COMBAT REPORT

Sector Serial No...(A)

Serial No. of Order detailing Flight or Squadron to
     Patrol...(B)

Date..(C)   **17·9. 41.**

Flight, Squadron...................................(D)   **Hurricane II.**
                                                 Flight: "A" Sqdn 81.

Number of Enemy Aircraft.......................(E)   **8**

Type of Enemy Aircraft...........................(F)   **Me.109.E.**

Time Attack was Delivered......................(G)   **1855.**

Place Attack was Delivered......................(H)   **Over enemy lines**
                                                 West. of Murmansk.

Height of Enemy.....................................(J)   **8000 ft.**

Enemy Casualties....................................(K)   **1 Me.109. Destroyed**

Our Casualties.............Aircraft.................(L)   **Nil.**
                        Personnel.............(M)

GENERAL REPORT............................(R)   **I was flying as Red 2.**
**Two 109's dived in front of the Squadron and Red 1 attacked the leader. I
followed and when Red 1 had finished his ammunition I attacked from
from the starboard quarter together with Black 1 on the port quarter. After
several short bursts for both of us pieces flew off E.A. and a large fire
started under the fuselage. E.A. then rolled over and dived into the
ground crashing by a small lake.**

Signature.................Sgt. 903466
                        Section   **Red**
OC   Flight   **"A"**
                        Squadron   Squadron No. **81.**
                        Signature of S/Ldr.

RAF Form1151

Top: A Hurricane IIB flies over Vayenga as another Hurricane, Z5227 from 81 Squadron, sits at readiness. Above: A quartet of 81 Squadron Hurricanes returns to Vayenga following a mission to escort Russian bombers attacking enemy front line positions. RAF

20.9.1941: At 15.25 hours three Hurricanes, Z4018 flown by F/Sgt. Haw, BD822 flown by Sgt. Carter and Z3768 flown by Sgt. Mulroy, took off for "Local Flying", landing back at Vayenga at 16.10.

At 16.55, Four Hurricanes, BD792 flown by S/Ldr. Rook, Z5228 flown by F/O. McGregor, Z5208 flown by P/O. Ramsey, and Z5209 flown by P/O. Walker, took off on an attempted interception of enemy aircraft. Four other Hurricanes, BD697 flown by F/Lt. Rook, Z3977 flown by Sgt. Reed, Z5207 flown by P/O. Bush and BD818 flown by P/O. Holmes, took off on patrol at 17.00 hours, all eight hurricanes from both flights landing back at 17.45, none having made contact with the enemy.

The supplement to Form 541 shows P/O. Holmes making a 10 minute practice flight at 18.20, landing at 18.30.

21.9.1941: At 09.50 hours three Hurricanes, BD818 flown by P/O. Holmes, Z5207 flown by Sgt. Crewe, and Z5227 flown by Sgt. Bishop, took off on practice flights, landing at 10.30. These are the only recorded No.81 Squadron sorties for this date; adverse weather prevailing.

23.9.1941: Four Hurricanes, BD792 flown by S/Ldr. Rook, Z5209 flown by P/O. Ramsey, Z3768 flown by Sgt. Sims and Z4018 flown by F/Sgt. Haw, took off at 15.50 hours on a patrol to attempt to intercept German aircraft, landing back at Vayenga at 17.10 without encountering any enemy aircraft. The supplement to Form 541 shows four other Hurricanes, BD697 flown by F/Lt. Rook, Z4006 flown by Sgt. Reed, BD818 flown by P/O. Holmes and Z5227 flown by P/O. Bush, taking off at 15.45 hours, five minutes earlier than the previously mentioned four; these aircraft landing at 17.10 hours along with the other flight.

24.9.1941: No.81 Squadron was tasked with flying its first mission to escort Russian bombers deep into enemy held territory. Six Hurricanes, BD792 flown by S/Ldr. Rook, Z4018 flown by F/Sgt. Haw, Z5228 flown by F/O. McGregor, BD822 flown by Sgt. Waud, Z5209 flown by P/O. Walker, and Z5157 flown by P/O. Ramsey, took off at 13.00 hours, landing back at Vayenga at 14.30. Another six Hurricanes, BD697 flown by F/Lt. Rook, Z3977 flown by P/O. Bush, Z5207 flown by Sgt. Anson, Z4006 flown by Sgt. Reed, Z5227 flown by P/O. Edmiston and BD818 flown by P/O. Holmes, took off at 13.05 hours, landing back at Vayenga at 14.20 hours. None of the flights encountered enemy aircraft.

26.9.1941: Three Hurricanes, Z5228 flown by F/O. McGregor, Z4018 flown by Sgt. Carter and Z5157 flown by Sgt. Mulroy, went up at 10.35 hours for some "Local Flying", landing back at 11.10.

Soviet pilots are shown around the cockpit of an 81 Squadron Hurricane IIB, during Hurricane conversion training for Soviet pilots. RAF

The Squadron was tasked with another bomber escort mission, six Hurricanes, BD792 flown by S/Ldr Rook, Z5228 flown by F/O. McGregor, Z4018 flown by F/Sgt. Haw, Z5209 flown by Sgt. Bishop, Z5157 flown by Sgt. Waud and Z3768 flown by Sgt. Sims, taking off at 17.55 hours (17.55 according to Form 541, but Form 540 states of the flight "airborne 18.05 hours". However, this was probably the time airborne of the last aircraft from the other flight of six Hurricanes, BD697 flown by F/Lt. Rook, BD818 flown by P/O. Holmes, Z4006 flown by Sgt. Reed, Z5217 flown by P/O. Edmiston, Z3977 flown by P/O. Bush and Z5207 flown by Sgt. Anson, which took off at 18.00 hours. Furthermore, Form 541 states initially only the first six aircraft and pilots mentioned above, a supplement providing details of the others. "… each flight of six machines escorting four bombers". During the escort mission 'B' Flight encountered German fighters, which attacked, with pilots noting that they observed "Cannon shell going past them". The Squadron record of the action reads:

"They then turned on the enemy aircraft which had dived from about 11,000 feet – one to two thousand feet above our formation. Blue 2 (Sgt. Reed turned and attacked his enemy aircraft from head-on, giving it two short bursts and another from above after rolling off his climb. After 150 rounds in all had been fired from each gun the enemy aircraft dived with black smoke pouring from it and crashed.

Two enemy aircraft attacked Green 2 (P/O. Edmiston) who dived away and then climbed to 8,000 feet when he saw an enemy aircraft pursuing Black 1. He then opened fire after diving about 4,000 feet and the bullets entered the enemy aircraft which then entered a cloud from which it was thought to crash but is still awaiting confirmation.

Green 1 (P/O. Holmes) also attacked a machine which was engaged with Black 1 and after closing in from 300 to 50 yards gave a two second deflection burst setting the enemy aircraft on fire after which it rolled over one and a half times and crashed. 25 rounds were fired from each gun. Black 1 (P/O. Bush) and Black 2 (Sgt. Anson) also fired their guns but without visible result."

By the end of the mission the Squadron had claimed three Me.109F's shot down. The first flight landed back at 18.45 hours and the second flight was down by 18.55 hours.

27.9.1941: No.81 Squadron was tasked with escorting four Russian bombers, Form 540 stating that "eight machines – four from each flight" took part. However, Form 541 records only seven Hurricanes, BD792 flown by S/Ldr. Rook, Z5228 flown by F/O. McGregor, Z5208 flown by P/O. Walker, Z5157 flown by P/O. Ramsey, Z4018 flown by F/Sgt. Haw, BD822 flown by Sgt. Waud and Z3768 flown by Sgt. Bishop; the first Flight taking off at 11.20 hours followed at 11.25 hours by the other Flight. However, A supplement to Form 541 adds details of a further five aircraft and pilots, Z5227 flown by P/O. Edmiston, BD697 flown by F/Lt. Rook, Z5207 flown by Sgt. Anson, Z3977 flown by P/O. Bush and Z4006 flown by Sgt. Reed, taking part in this mission, taking off at 11.20 hours. It is determined, therefore, that 12 aircraft - 2 flights of 6 aircraft each - actually took part in this mission.

The Squadron encountered German Me.109's at 1200 hours. "Flight Sergeant Haw was White leader in the Flight formation when four ME.109's(E) attacked. The leader of their Section 2 attempted a beam attack on White leader who turned towards him and after three complete turns got on his tail giving him several short bursts. The enemy aircraft then crashed in flames."

"P/O Edmiston was Blue 3 in 'B' Flight and made a stern attack on an ME.109F from which the hood came away after 40 rounds from each gun had been fired. The enemy aircraft then spun into the ground."

At the conclusion of the mission the Squadron aircraft returned to base, landing between 12.25 and 12.45 hours, with the exception of Sgt, Anson in Z5207, who laded back at 11.35, having returned with a fault.

At 13.40 hours, S/Ldr. Rook in BD792,, P/O. Walker in Z5209, Sgt. Bishop in Z3768, P/O. Ramsey in Z5157, F/Sgt. Haw in Z4018 and Sgt. Waud in BD822, took off on an "aerodrome defence" mission at 1340, landing at 1445.

28.9.1941: At 15.45 hours S/Ldr. Rook flying BD792 and P/O. Walker flying Z5209, took off from Vayenga on an attempted interception of German aircraft, landing at 16.40.

The Squadron was again tasked with escorting Russian bombers and at 17.15 hours six Hurricanes, BD792 flown by S/Ldr. Rook, Z5209 flown by P/O. Walker, BD822 flown by Sgt. Waud, Z5157 flown by P/O. Ramsey, Z5228 flown by F/O. McGregor and Z3768 flown by Sgt. Sims, took off, landing back at 18.15.

At 17.10 hours, five minutes before the first above mentioned flight took off, six Hurricanes were launched to provide "High Cover", BD697 flown by F/Lt. Rook, Z4006 flown by Sgt. Reed, BD818 flown by P/O. Holmes, Z3977 flown by P/O. Bush, Z5207 flown by Sgt. Anson and Z5227 flown by Sgt. Crewe, taking off at 17.10, landing back at Vayenga at 18.20 hours.

Only one sortie is recorded for 29 September, Sgt. Reed flying Z4006 on an air test, taking off at 09.20 and landing back at 09.30 hours. No sorties are recorded for the 30th.

During September, No.81 Squadron recorded 184 flying hours; this including the flights by the twelve Squadron Hurricanes that flew off from HMS *Argus* and the flight times of the seven aircraft flown in from Archangel. The Squadron had claimed 12 enemy aircraft destroyed, and a 13th probably destroyed, but unconfirmed, for the lost of one Hurricane. However, The Squadron Hurricane establishment was down to 17 aircraft by the end of the month as one of the aircraft had been painted up in Soviet Red Star colours and presented to "The Russian General for his own use". Of the seventeen Hurricanes, some of them still had no workable guns, while others were without their full complement of guns. The Squadron recorded no accidents and had only a single noted sortie abort.

Of the twelve enemy aircraft confirmed shot down, it was noted that ten were brought down by pilots brought over from No.504 Squadron, while the other two were shot down by pilots brought over from 402 and 123 Squadrons.

No.81 Squadron Hurricane IIB Z4017 runs up its engine as it prepares for take-off on a sortie from Vayenga. RAF

Adverse weather conditions meant there was practically no flying conducted during the first six days of October; a handful of non-operational flights were conducted on the 1ˢᵗ of the month. S/Ldr. Rook taking BD792 up on an air test at 10.35 hours, landing at 11.00. F/O. McGregor went aloft in Z5228 in an airframe test flight at 15.50 hours; landing at 16.05, and Sgt, Carter flew Z3768 in an R.D.F. test flight at 17.30, landing at 18.20.

6.10.1941: Four Hurricanes, BD792 flown by S/Ldr. Rook, Z5228 flown by F/O. McGregor, Z5209 flown by P/O. Walker and Z5157 flown by P/O. Ramsey, took off for "Local Flying" training at 11.20 hours, S/Ldr. Rook landing back at 11.25 and the other three landing at 11.55. Another Hurricane, Z3977 flown by P/O. Bush, had taken off on a practice flight at 11.15, landing at 11.55.

Vayenga aerodrome was attacked by 12 Luftwaffe Ju.88 bombers operating from Northern Norway. It appeared that these aircraft had been dispatched to

North Norway from Holland around a month before for anti-shipping operations, but the severe arctic weather conditions had severely curtailed these operations. 151 Wing at Vayenga received advanced notice that 14 Ju.88's had departed their base in Norway with the intention of attacking Vayenga, two apparently aborting. This formation was to join up with an escort of 6 Me.109's, but the rendezvous never took place and the bombers continued unescorted.

The advance information received about the attack allowed 151 Wing to prepare to intercept the formation, with eight Hurricanes of 81 Squadron and six from 134 Squadron being launched on aerodrome patrol.

No. 81 Squadron aircraft and pilot take off and landing times for the 6 October combats were as follows:

Z3768 (Sgt. Sims) take-off	16.00	16.30	
BD822 (Sgt. Bishop) take off	16.00	16.30	
BD792 (S/Ldr. Rook) take off	16.00	16.30 (supplement to Form 541
shows F/Lt. Rook taking off at 16.00 and landing at 16.40) Defensive Patrol
Z5228 (F/O. McGregor) take off	16.00	16.30	
Z5209 (P/O. Walker)	16.00	16.30	
Z5157 P/O. Ramsey	16.00	16.30	
Z4006 (Sgt. Crewe)	16.00	16.30	Defensive Patrol
Z3977 (P/O. Bush)	16.10	17.20	Defensive Patrol
BD818 (P/O. Holmes)	16.10	16.25	Defensive Patrol
Z44018 (F/Sgt. Haw)	16.30	16.45	
BD792 (S/Ldr. Rook)	16.45	17.30	
Z5157 (P/O. Ramsey)	16.45	17.30	
Z3768 (Sgt. Sims)	16.45	17.30	
Z5209 (P/O. Walker)	16.45	17.30	

81 Squadron Narrative of the 6 October combats reproduced verbatim.

1605 "The C.O attacked No.3 in a formation of six JU.88's and spun away after a two second burst (quarter to stern) when one engine was u/s. He then intercepted a JU.88 with P/O. Furneaux (134 Squadron)and after beam attacks, the E/A crashed.

Red 2 (P/O. Ramsey attacked No.3 in the enemy aircraft formation after the C.O. had broken away and fired a three second burst. Black and white smoke was then pouring from the port engine. Red 2 then attacked another JU.88 giving it a quarter stern burst and several further short bursts at close range down to ground level. An A/C of 134 Squadron also fired a short burst at this machine.

When the ammunition of Red 2 was exhausted he returned to base.

White leader (P/O. Walker) attacked No.6 in the E/A formation at about 7,000 feet giving it a stern burst at 400 yards slowing it up and setting the port engine on fire. Three more attacks were made 300 to 50 yards and after the second attack no return fire was received and the enemy was making for the ground. At 2,500 rounds Red (illegible, but probably Red 2) had stoppages and had to return to base."

At 16.10 " White 2 (Sgt. Bishop) attacked a JU.88 from below at about 300 yards and then attacked again from astern and below when smoke appeared from the starboard engine. The enemy aircraft was then intercepted by two more Hurricanes and when last seen was going to ground in a spiral dive. There was no return fire.

Yellow leader (P/O. McGregor) opened fire on No.3 in the enemy formation but broke off leaving it to Red Section. He then dived on a JU.88 about 6,000 feet below and carried out a starboard beam attack from 400 to 200 yards giving it two bursts of two seconds and following up with two port quarter attacks, hitting in the neighbourhood of both engines. The enemy aircraft was last seen flying down a valley at ground level with its port engine burning furiously."

1620 "Blue 1 (F/Lt. Rook) was weaving behind 'A' Flight but joined a Hurricane in chasing a JU.88 at ground level getting in a short burst (quarter stern) at 250 yards. He then chased two more JU.88's but lost them at ground level, next meeting six aircraft in pair's line astern and stepped down. These he thought to be Hurricanes of No.134 Squadron and joined in a left-hand climbing turn with them, level with the centre section but not close enough to see their markings.

At the cloud base, 8,000 feet, the leader of the centre section 'peeled off' and flew straight at Blue 1 who noticed the yellow nose in time and opened fire from 250 yards to 50 yards shooting down the ME. On being attacked by the other ME.109's he took evasive action and returned to base. Blue 2 (Sgt. Crewe) fired his guns without visible effect.

The remaining three machines of 'B' Flight were ordered to take off shortly before the JU.88's arrived over the aerodrome and P/O's Bush and Holmes got off the ground but the engine of P/O. Edmiston's plane stalled when two bombs dropped possibly aimed at the 'B' Flight planes. P/O. Bush's machine had a bullet through the windscreen and four dents in the fuselage and P/O. Holmes machine had a bullet through the fuselage and a piece out of the propeller. P/O. Edmiston's machine had a piece out of the tailplane. The two machines did aerodrome patrol but saw nothing."

The Combats of the 6th were the last major operation for 81 Squadron in Russia. On the 7th, there was only a single recorded sortie, BD697 flown by Sgt. Anson on a 15 minute air test, taking off at 07.45 and landing at 08.00. On the 8th, 3 Hurricanes, BD818 flown by P/O. Holmes, Z4006 flown by Sgt. Reed and Z5227 flown by P/O. Edmiston, took off on a patrol at 12.00 hours, landing back at 12.20. These three sorties were the last operational sorties for 81 Squadron flying their own aircraft, but the pilots would later fly operations using No.134 Squadron aircraft.

Ground crew preparing to start an 81 Squadron Hurricane IIB at a snow covered Vayenga aerodrome. RAF

During the course of October, No.81 Squadron had flown 35 hours and 40 minutes. The Squadron had claimed 13 and a half enemy aircraft destroyed for the loss of one Hurricane since operations had commenced in North Russia the previous month.

On 15 October, Soviet Air Force pilots took possession of the Hurricanes of 'A' Flight No.81 Squadrons, flying six sorties in them that day, totaling 3 hours and 15 minutes flying time.

On the 22nd, the remaining 81 Squadron Hurricanes were taken over by the Soviet Air Force; 81 Squadron pilots officially ending operations in North Russia. However, some Squadron ground personnel continued operating with the New Soviet No.1 Hurricane Squadron.

NO.134 SQUADRON OPERATIONS – SEPTEMBER AND OCTOBER 1941

11.9.1941: No 134 Squadron commenced operations on this date when four Hurricanes of "B" Flight, Z3978 flown by P/O. Cameron, Z5159 flown by P/O. Furneaux, Z5210 flown by F/Sgt. McCann and Z3763 flown by F/Lt. Ross (Flight Leader), took off on a Sector Recce at 13.35 hours. Although recorded as a Recce, this was more a familiarization flight to acquaint the pilots with the operational area. The flight was led by a Soviet Air Force "I-20" fighter flown by Captain Kuharenko, who took the Hurricanes on a patrol from "Murmansk, East to the Finnish frontier, approx. 40 miles along the frontier to the sea, Northward, thence East back to Vayenga". During the flight the Hurricanes tested their guns, landing back at Vayenga at 14.35. No enemy aircraft were encountered, but the mission was not without drama as two Hurricanes, "Z3763 flown by F/Lt. Ross and Z3978 flown by P/O. Cameron "cut out three times over enemy territory, and the pilots were gliding to ground, when the engines picked up at a few hundred feet". It was determined that inferior fuel supplied by the Soviets was to blame as no faults could be found with the aircraft when they landed.

Four Hurricanes of 'A' Flight, Z5205 flown by S/Ldr. Miller, Z5253 flown by F/Lt. Berg, BD699 flown by Sgt. Clarke and Z4013 flown by P/O. Sheldon, took-off on a Sector Recce at 14.15 hours. This was a similar patrol to that flown by 'B' Flight earlier, again led by a Soviet "I-20" fighter. Two of the Hurricanes developed engine trouble almost immediately, aborting and returned to the field. Z5253 (F/Lt. Berg) landing at 14.40 and Z4013 (P/O. Sheldon) landing at 14.45. The remaining two aircraft continued with the patrol, landing back at base at 15.05.

12.9.1941: Z3978 flown by P/O. Cameron took off on an air test at 10.15, landing at 10.40. The first patrol of the day was launched when three Hurricanes from 'B' Flight, Z3763 (F/Lt. Ross), Z3978 (P/O. Cameron) and Z5210 (F/Sgt. McCann) took off at 11.15, landing back between 12.20 and 12.35. Another

Hurricane, Z5159 (P/O. Elkington), had taken off at 10.55 and landed at 11.25. It is unclear if this was planned as part of the above mentioned patrol. It is listed in the operational records as being on a "Recco Patrol", distinct from the other three aircraft being listed as on a "Front Line Patrol".

'A' Flight launched three Hurricanes, Z5205 (F/Lt. Berg), BD699 (P/O. Furneaux) and Z5123 (P/O. Sheldon), on a Front Line Patrol; Z5205 taking off at 11.55, while the other two had taken off five minutes earlier. This patrol proved uneventful; BD699 landing at 13.20, Z5123 landing at 13.35 and Z5205 landing at 13.55.

Three Hurricanes were launched by 'B' Flight, Z5159 (P/O. Cameron) at 17.25, Z3763 (F/Sgt. Barnes) and Z5210 (F/Sgt. McCann) at 17.35, these aircraft landing at 18.30. Two Hurricanes from 'A' Flight, BD699 (P/O. Furneaux) and Z5123 (P/O. Sheldon), were launched on a base patrol flight at 17.25, landing at 18.20 and 18.35 hours

The Squadron records for the 12th recorded "'B' Flight whilst on patrol sighted and chased 3 ME 110's over Murmansk Naval Base. Both sections surrounded by heavy A.A. fire from ground and broke away. No contact with enemy".

Six additional Hurricanes for No.134 Squadron arrived at Afrikanda aerodrome at 14.30 hours, having departed Archangel at 12.30. These aircraft and pilots consisted of BD825 (P/O. Wollaston), Z5226 (Sgt. Griffiths), BD790 (Sgt. Fry), Z5236 (Sgt. Kirvan), Z4012 (Sgt. Knapton) and Z5123 (Sgt. Kiel). Four of these Hurricanes, BD825 (P/O. Wollaston), Z5236 (Sgt. Kirvan), Z4012 (Sgt. Knapton and Z5123 (Sgt. Kiel), departed Afrikanda at 17.30, landing at Vayenga at 19.15 hours. The other two Hurricanes, Z5226 (Sgt. Griffiths) and BD790 (Sgt. Fry) took off from Afrikanda at 13.30 hours on the 13th, and landed at Vayenga at 14.15 hours.

13.9.1941: P/O. Furneaux took Hurricane Z5253 up for an air test at 10.55, landing at 11.10.

Four Hurricanes from 'A' Flight, Z5205 (S/Ldr. Miller), BD699 (Sgt. Clarke), Z5123 (Sgt. Campbell) and Z5134 (Sgt. Gould) took off, in fine weather, between 13.43 and 13.45 on a Base Security Patrol, escorting Soviet bomber aircraft into Vayenga aerodrome. Sgt. Gould took Z5134 up again at 16.40 on a 15 minute air test, landing at 16.55.

Another base patrol of four Hurricanes was flown by 'A' flight, Z5205 (F/Lt. Berg), Z5253 (P/O. Furneaux), Z5123 (P/O. Sheldon) and BD699 (Sgt. Kirvan), taking off at 17.10 and landing at 17.50. There is some uncertainly about which patrol escorted the Soviet bombers into Vayenga, this one or the earlier patrol flown by 'A' Flight at 13.45, or both.

'B' Flight flew a base patrol of four Hurricanes, Z3763 (F/Lt. Ross), Z3978 (F/Sgt. Barnes), Z5159 (P/O. Wollaston) and Z5120 (Sgt. Knapton), taking off at 14.00, landing at 15.05.

No.134 Squadron Hurricane IIB ZE159 GV 33 in its dispersal at Vayenga. The Soviets used "natural material" to camouflage the dispersal areas. RAF

14.9.1941: The Wing received reports of a formation of 39 Ju-88 bombers escorted by 11 Me.109's (Squadron Form 541 states the escort to be 11 Me.110's). Four Hurricanes from 'A' Flight, Z5205 (S/Ldr. Miller), Z5253 (Sgt. Gould), BD699 (Sgt. Campbell) and Z5123 (P/O. Sheldon), took off on patrol at 13.55 in the hope of intercepting the enemy formation. 'B' Flight launched three aircraft, Z3763 (F/Lt. Ross), Z5159 (F/Sgt. Barnes) and Z5210 (Sgt. Griffiths). The Hurricanes patrolled No.2 Zone, but did not make contact with the enemy aircraft. 'A' Flight landed at 15.00 and 'B' Flight landed at 15.05.

15.9.1941: Nine German bombers were reported in the area of responsibility and ten Hurricanes were lunched to intercept. 'B' Flight Hurricanes Z3763 (F/Lt. Ross), Z5139 (P/O. Cameron), Z5120 (F/Sgt. Barnes), Z5210 (Sgt. Gould) and Z4012 (Sgt. Knapton), took off at 10.45 hours to patrol "No.2 Line, Zone 2". 'A' Flight, Hurricanes, Z5205 (S/Ldr. Miller), BD825 (F/Lt. Berg), Z5123 (P/O. Sheldon), BD699 (Sgt. Clarke) and Z5203 (Sgt. Campbell), taking off at 10.50 to patrol Zone 2. The Hurricanes patrolled at 11,000 ft, which was just below the cloud base, but neither Flight made contact with the enemy aircraft. A smoke pall was noted over the "vicinity of bulge in front towards Murmansk". 'B' Flight landed at 11.45 and 'A' Flight landed at 11.50.

Another patrol was sent over Murmansk in the afternoon, nine Hurricanes being involved. Hurricanes Z5159 (P/O. Wollaston), Z5210 (F/Sgt. McCann) and Z5120 (Sgt. Fry) of 'B' Flight took off at 15.45. Hurricanes BD825 (Sgt. Campbell), Z5253 (P/O. Furneaux) and BD699 (Sgt. Clarke), took off at 15.50 and Z5205 (S/Ldr. Miller) took off at 16.05. These aircraft were to patrol the Murmansk area at 2,000 ft. No enemy aircraft were encountered and the aircraft landed at 16.35 (Sgt. Campbell in BD825 returned at 16.25 with a rough engine, which was overheating.

At 18.40 four Hurricanes from 'A' Flight, Z5205 (F/Lt. Berg), Z5253 (P/O. Furneaux), BD699 (Sgt. Gould) and Z5125 (Sgt. Kirvan), took off and patrolled with No.81 Squadron aircraft in No.2 Line, which was in the southern area of Zone 2. This patrol, conducted at 6,000 ft, encountered no enemy aircraft and the Squadrons returned, 'A' Flight No.134 Squadron landing at 1925.

At 12.00 F/Lt. Berg took Hurricane BD825 up on an air test, landing at 12.20. He again took BD825 up on an air test at 17.40, landing at 18.10 At 17.35 two Hurricanes, Z5159 (F/Sgt. Barnes) and Z4012 (Sgt. Fry) took off on practice flights, which included mock dog-fighting, landing at 18.20.

Form 540 records that Sgt. Kirvan landed Hurricane Z4013 "on soft patch causing undercarriage to buckle and machine piled up in ground". However, Form 541 shows Sgt. Kirvan flying Hurricane Z5125. Squadron records show no flight by Z4013 on the 15th. Z5123 was not flown again until it was taken up on an air test on 20 September.

16.9.1941: There was no operational flying, but one and a half hours of practice flying were conducted. The Squadron received three new Hurricanes, Z5211 flown by Sgt. Griffiths, Z5303 flown by Sgt. Douglas and Z5723 flown by Sgt. Kiel, taking off from Archangel at 15.15 hours, landing at Afrikanda at 16.10; departing Afrikanda at 17.00 and arriving at Vayenga at 18.00.

17.9.1941: Four Hurricanes from 'B' Flight, BD825 (F/Lt. Berg), Z5236 (P/O. Elkington), Z5253, P/O. Furneaux) and BD699 (Sgt. Clarke), along with five Hurricanes from 'A' Flight, Z4012 (S/Ldr. Miller), Z3763 (F/Lt. Ross), Z5159 (P/O. Wollaston), Z5120 (F/Sgt. Barnes) and Z5210 (Sgt. Griffiths), took off at 11.55 hours to patrol No.2 Patrol Line. No enemy aircraft were encountered and both flights landed back at 13.05, with the exception of Sgt. Clarke of 'B' Flight who landed at 12.55.

At 16.35 two Hurricanes, Z5236 (P/O. Elkington) and BD699 (Sgt. Kiel), took off on what is conflictingly described in various squadron records as an "Air Test" and a "Recco", both aircraft landing at 17.05. Another Hurricane, Z5206 (S/Ldr. Miller) took off on an air test at 16.55, landing at 17.05.

Three Hurricanes, Z3978 (P/O. Griffiths), BD790 (Sgt. Douglas) and Z4012 (Sgt. Fry), took off at 16.15, landing at 17.15. There is nothing clear in the Squadron records to denote what these sorties were, but considering that the two Sgt. Pilots had arrived at Vayenga only the day before, it is reasonable to conclude that these were practice flights.

Nine No.134 Squadron Hurricanes were again launched to patrol No.2 Patrol Line in the evening. Z5159 (P/O. Cameron), BD790 (Sgt. Griffiths), Z4012 (Sgt. Knapton), Z5120 (F/Sgt. Barnes) and Z5210 (F/Sgt. McCann), taking off at 18.55. Z5206 (S/Ldr. Miller) and BD825 (F/Lt. Berg) took off at 19.05 and Z5236 (P/O. Elkington) and BD699 (Sgt. Gould) took off at 19.10. The Squadron was tasked to patrol No.2 Patrol Line at 6,000 ft, but did not encounter any enemy aircraft and landed back at Vayenga between 19.35 and 19.40 hours. No.81 Squadron shot down 3 Me.109's, during an earlier patrol.

18.9.1941: The showery, partially cloudy weather of the previous few changed to freezing snow and sleet, sometimes turning to rain. There was no operational flying. Two Hurricanes Z5205 (S/Ldr. Miller) and Z5120 (F/Sgt. Barnes), flew weather test sorties from 10.20 to 10.30 and 16.40 to 17.00 hours respectively.

19.9.1941: The snow and rain led to the field being all but unserviceable and some areas completely waterlogged. There was a taxing accident when Hurricane Z5226 (Sgt. Griffiths) started to taxi, but sank in sand after a distance of only 10 - 15 yards. The Hurricane "tipped nose into sand breaking airscrew".

At 11.30 P/O. Furneaux took Z5253 up on an air test (also recorded in some records as a weather test), landing at 11.40.

Five Hurricanes, Z4012 (P/O. Cameron), Z5120 (F/Sgt. Barnes), Z5159 (P/O. Wollaston), Z5210 (F/Sgt. McCann) and BD790 (Sgt, Douglas), were scrambled at 18.45 hours, landing at 19.35. These were the only operational sorties flown by the Squadron this day.

20.9.1941: The Squadron was tasked with patrolling No. 1 Zone, Line 2 in the afternoon. Ten Hurricanes, Z5205 (S/Ldr. Miller), BD825 (F/Lt. Berg), Z5236 (P/O. Elkington), Z5283 (P/O. Furneaux), BD699 (Sgt. Kiel), Z5120 (P/O. Cameron), BD790 (Sgt. Douglas), Z4012 (Sgt. Knapton), Z5763 (P/O. Wollaston) and Z5210 (P/O. Sheldon), took off at 16.20. During the patrol no enemy aircraft were noted, however, the Hurricanes investigated aircraft that turned out to be Soviet. Unlike previous patrols, this patrol was flown in an anti-clockwise direction. The only enemy action noted was "Two puffs of German ac ac, observed, accurate range and height (2500 ft)". Although the weather was stormy in places, generally it was around 6/10ths cloud with good visibility. The Squadron landed back a base at 17.30, during which Sgt Griffiths in Hurricane Z5210 "over shot landing ground into ditch on perimeter breaking airscrew, causing left undercarriage gear to collapse".

Hurricane Z5253 (P/O. Furneaux) was flown on an air test; take off at 13.45 and landing at 14.00. Another Hurricane, Z5123 (P/O. Sheldon) took off on an air test at 17.05, landing at 17.55.

No.134 Squadron Hurricane IIB's being scrambled at a snow covered Vayenga aerodrome. RAF

21-23.9.1941: The weather was showery with several instances of low lying storm cloud. The aerodrome was again largely unserviceable. During the night 21/22 September, some two inches of snow fell. The thaw the following day, combined with further heavy snow showers, turned the field to mud, curtailing any flying. A further three inches of snow apparently fell during the night of 22/23 September. There was no scheduled flying, but No.134 Squadron was brought to readiness at 16.00 hours following reports of "enemy aircraft crossing the front"; stood down later.

Guarded by Soviet sentries, No.134 Squadron Hurricane IIB Z5253 GA 25, taxis from its dispersal prior to take off. RAF

24.9.1941: The snow of the previous few days had thawed, leaving behind fine clear weather over Vayenga, although over enemy territory there was considerable cloud. Only one patrol was flown to escort 3 Soviet bombers over No.1 Line. Twelve Hurricanes, Z5205 (S/Ldr. Miller), Z5253 (P/O. Furneaux), BD825 (F/Lt. Berg), Z5236 (P/O. Elkington), BD699 (Sgt. Clarke), Z5134 (Sgt. Gould), Z3763 (F/Lt. Ross), Z5120 (F/Sgt. Barnes), Z5226 (F/Sgt. McCann), Z4012 (Sgt. Fry), Z3978 (P/O. Cameron) and BD790 (Sgt. Knapton), taking off at 10.55 hours. No enemy aircraft were encountered, but the Squadron reported "heavy anti aircraft fire". 'A' Flight landed between 10.05 and 12.10 hours, while 'B' Flight landed between 11.55 and 12.00, with the exception of Z4102 (Sgt, Fry), which landed at 11.15. Two of the Hurricanes, BD699 (Sgt. Clarke) and Z5134 (Sgt. Gould) had just landed from an air test at 10.55, having taken off at 10.00 hours.

Hurricane Z5303 (Sgt. Campbell) was flown on an air test at 14.00 hours, landing at 14.10. Another Hurricane, Z4012 (Sgt. Knapton) took off on an air test at 14.00 hours, landing at 14.40. A weather test flight was flown by

Hurricane Z5236 (P/O. Elkington) at 16.45, landing at 16.55.

25.9.1941: No Flying by No.134 Squadron

26.9.1941: S/Ldr. Miller flew an air test in Z5205, taking off at 09.50 and landing at 10.05. During the landing the aircraft "ran through a wet patch of sand, causing heavy splashing, which damaged wing flaps".

No.134 Squadron launched 12 Hurricanes, Z5205 (S/Ldr. Miller), BD825 (F/Lt. Berg), Z5303 (Sgt. Campbell), BD699 (Sgt. Clarke), Z5236 (P/O. Elkington), Z3978 (P/O. Cameron), Z4012 (Sgt. Fry), BD790 (Sgt. Douglas), Z5226 (F/Sgt. McCann) and Z5120 F/Sgt. Barnes), taking off at 12.40, while Z5123 (Sgt. Kiel) took off at 12.45. The 12th aircraft is not listed in From 541 and S/Ldr Millers flight is listed as an air test, but is understood to be part of the patrol. The Squadron patrolled No.4 Line to intercept enemy bombers that had been reported heading towards Vayenga. No enemy aircraft were encountered and the Squadron landed between 13.25 and 13.40 hours, with the exception of Z5123 (Sgt. Kiel), who landed at 13.00.

As noted above, S/Ldr. Millers aircraft, ZD5205, was damaged in the morning, but is also listed in Form 541 as having flown in the afternoon on an "Air Test". However, it is assumed that this is an error and the aircraft was flown on the attempted interception of enemy bombers probably following an air test, which is supported by other operational documents.

During the day Soviet Pilots flew practice flights in 134 Squadron Hurricanes. Captain Safonov (Soviet Air Force) flew in Hurricane Z4012, which was damaged during landing when the aircraft (ran through waterlogged patches of sand and heavy splashing damaged wing flaps". Captain Kuharenko (Soviet Air Force) flew Hurricane Z5211 on a practice flight, taking off at 17.15 and landing at 17.40. Squadron records noted that the "take off was bad but landing perfect". Two 134 Hurricanes, Z3763 (F/Lt. Ross) and Z5159 (P/O. Cameron), were launched along with Captain Kuharenko at 17.15, conducting a patrol and landing at 18.20.

27.9.1941: The Squadron flew six operations. Six Hurricanes of 'B' Flight were ordered to patrol No.1 Zone "well over battle front". The aircraft, Z5159 (S/Ldr. Miller), Z4012 (Sgt. Knapton), Z3763 (F/Lt. Ross), Z5226 (F/Sgt. McCann), BD790 (P/O. Cameron) and Z5120 (F/Sgt. Barnes), took off at 07.20 hours. No enemy aircraft were encountered, but heavy anti aircraft fire was encountered over the battle front. During this patrol BD790 (P/O. Cameron) conducted a strafing attack on a wooded section of the front. However, no Squadron records indicate what he was attacking. The aircraft returned to base and all landed by 08.35.

A similar patrol was flown over No.1 Patrol Line by six Hurricanes of 'A' Flight. The aircraft, BD825 (F/Lt. Berg), Z5253 (P/O. Furneaux), BD699 (Sgt.

Kiel), Z5236 (Sgt. Kirvan), Z5134 (Sgt. Gould) and Z5303 (Sgt. Campbell), taking off at 08.30. This patrol followed "4 Soviet bombers at a distance", encountering heavy anti aircraft fire, but encountered no enemy aircraft. 'A' Flight landed at 09.20.

At 11.50 seven Hurricanes of 'B' Flight, Z5159 (S/Ldr. Miller), Z4012 (Sgt. Knapton), Z3763 (F/Lt. Ross), Z5226 (Sgt McCann), BD790 (P/O. Cameron), Z5120 (F/Sgt. Barnes) and Z5211 (Sgt. Douglas), took off to provide top cover at 15,000 ft for six 'A' Flight Hurricanes escorting Soviet Bombers attacking front line positions. The 'A' Flight aircraft Hurricanes, BD825 (F/Lt. Berg), Z5253 (P/O. Furneaux), Z5134 (Sgt. Gould), Z5236 (Sgt. Kiel), BD699 (Sgt. Clarke), Z5123 (P/O. Sheldon) and Z5303 (P/O. Cameron), took off at 12.00. The disparity in numbers – 7 from each flight – was due to one Sgt. Pilot from 'B' Flight joining 'A' Flight. The Soviet "P.2" bombers being escorted attacked anti aircraft positions on the front line. An Me.109 with a yellow nose was observed heading due West, and P/O. Sheldon "endeavoured to catch but failed to make contact..." The Squadrons Hurricanes landed at 13.00.

The Wing received a report that A Ju.88 bomber was heading for Vayenga aerodrome and five Hurricanes, 3 from 'A' Flight and 2 from 'B' Flight. The two 'B' Flight Hurricanes, Z3768 (P/O. Cameron) and BD790 (P/O. Wollaston, were scrambled at 15.00 hours, followed by the three 'A' Flight Hurricanes, BD699 (Sgt. Clarke), Z5253 (P/O. Furneaux) and BD825 (F/Lt. Berg), which were scrambled at 15.10. None of the Hurricanes managed to intercept the Ju.88, which apparently circled Vayenga aerodrome twice at an altitude of 12,000 ft before leaving.

Tragedy struck when one of the 'A' Flight Hurricanes, BD825 (F/Lt. Berg) took off during the scramble with two airmen, AC2 Ridley and AC2 Thomas, still sitting on the tailplane, "the pilot having apparently overlooked that they were on the tail. At approximately 50 feet the aircraft stalled and crashed becoming a total wreck. F/Lt. Berg sustained serious injuries; AC2 Ridley and AC2 Thomas were killed instantaneously". P/O. Cameron was given temporary command of 'A' Flight following the accident, as F/Lt. Berg was hospitalised with serious injuries.

Eight 'B' Flight Hurricanes, Z3763 (F/Lt. Ross), Z5211 (Sgt. Fry), Z3978 (P/O. Cameron), Z5159 (Sgt. Knapton), Z5226 (F/Sgt. McCann), Z5120 (F/Sgt. Barnes), BD790 (P/O. Wollaston) and Z5134 (Sgt. Douglas), took off at 16.50 to escort Soviet "twin tailed SB" bombers attacking front line positions from 5,000 ft. No enemy aircraft were encountered. The Flight landed at 17.50.

Six Hurricanes from 'B' Flight, Z5205 (S/Ldr. Miller), BD699 (Sgt. Clarke), Z5253 (P/O. Furneaux), Z5236 (Sgt. Kiel), Z5123 (P/O. Sheldon) and Z5303 (Sgt. Campbell), took off at 18.15 to patrol No's 1, 2 and 3 Zones at 3,000 ft in an attempt to intercept enemy fighters reported to be attacking Soviet bombers. However, no enemy aircraft were encountered and the flight landed between 18.45 and 18.50.

Pilots walk to the post mission debrief by the Intelligence Officer following a mission escorting Russian bombers attacking front line positions. A No.134 Squadron Hurricane IIB is about to refueled in the background. RAF

There were two practice flights with Soviet pilots, Captain Savanov taking off in Hurricane Z5134 at 17.50, landing at 1830 and Captain Kuharenko taking off in the same aircraft at around 18.30, landing at 18.45.

28.9.1941: Six Hurricanes of 'A' Flight, Z5205 (S/Ldr. Miller), Z5303 (Sgt. Campbell), Z5253 (P/O. Furneaux), BD699 (Sgt. Kirvan), Z5236 (P/O. Elkington) and Z5134 (Sgt. Gould), took off at 12.40 to patrol Zone 4 at 8,000 ft and provide escort to Soviet bombers. During the patrol "Flashes were reported at Polyano Naval Base", but were not observed by the Hurricane pilots, possibly due to low cloud. The aircraft landed at 13.35.

At 17.35 Hurricanes of 'B' Flight, Z3763 (F/Lt. Ross), Z5226 (Sgt. Fry), Z5120 (F/Sgt. Barnes), Z5159 (P/O. Wollaston) and Z4012 (Sgt. Knapton), took off. Five minutes later Hurricanes of 'A' Flight, Z3978 (P/O. Cameron), Z5303 (Sgt. Kiel), Z5253 (P/O. Furneaux), Z5123 (P/O. Sheldon) and BD699 (Sgt. Clarke), took off. Conflicting Squadron records record that 12 aircraft were involved, but Form 541 shows only the 11 recorded above. The Squadron was tasked to escort 4 Soviet bombers, which were attacking a column of German troops moving up to front line positions. 'B' Flight were tasked to provide close escort at an altitude of 8,000 ft, while 'A' Flight were flying top cover at 10,000 ft, slightly above a thin cloud layer. The Squadron observed the Soviet bombs dropping and anti-aircraft fire, which was apparently directed at No.81 Squadron Hurricanes. No enemy aircraft were encountered and the Squadron landed between 18.40 and 19.00.

29.9.1941: At 17.05, six 'A' Flight Hurricanes, Z3978 (P/O. Cameron), Z5303 (Sgt. Campbell), Z5123 (P/O. Sheldon), Z5211 (Sgt. Kirvan), BD699 (Sgt. Clarke) and Z5134 (Sgt. Gould), took off to patrol No.1 Patrol Line, Zone 1 at an altitude of 4,000 ft to provide air cover for a Soviet Navy Destroyer bombarding enemy positions. At 17.50 'B' Flight launched 5 Hurricanes, Z5159 (P/O. Wollaston), Z5120 (F/Sgt. Barnes), Z5226 (F/Sgt. McCann), Z5236 (P/O. Elkington) and BD790 (Sgt. Fry), along with a single Hurricane from 'A' Flight, Z5253 (P/O. Furneaux). This Flight was tasked to provide escort to 3 Soviet "P.2" bombers, which were attacking front line positions. 'B' Flight covered the bombers at an altitude of 10,000 ft. Due to haze obscuring the ground the bombers did not release their loads and the bombers and escorting Hurricanes overflew the Russian Destroyer bombarding front line positions. The Destroyer and two small anti aircraft vessels opened fire, hitting one of the P.2's, which then jettisoned its bombs close to the Destroyer. The crew of the Soviet aircraft bailed out and the aircraft crashed in the vicinity of Vayenga aerodrome. 'B' Flight landed at Vayenga at 18.45, 'A' Flight having landed half an hour earlier.

At 11.55, Z4012 was flown on an Air Test by Sgt. Griffiths, landing at 12.25. There were two Soviet practice flights, Z4012 (Captain Savonov) taking off at 16.50, landing at 17.30. Captain Kukarenko then took this aircraft up around 17.30, landing at 18.10. Z5253 was flown on a weather test by P/O. Furneaux; taking off at 20.10 and landing at 22.20.

1.10.1941: There was no operational flying by the Squadron. Sgt. Kiel took Z5211 up on a weather test flight at 08.35, landing at 08.45. Two Hurricanes, Z5123 (P/O. Sheldon) and BD699 (Sgt. Clarke), took off at 15.10 hours for formation flying practice. There were two practice flights by Soviet pilots utilising Hurricane Z4012. Captain Savanov taking off at 16.35, landing at 17.05; Captain Kuharenko then taking the aircraft up, landing at 17.35.

P/O. Cameron took over command of 'A' Flight, with effect from the 27 September, the date he had assumed temporary command of the Flight following the accident and injury to F/Lt. Berg.

2.10.1941: Low cloud wiped out any planned operations. A planned attack on a town in Finland by Soviet "P.2" bombers was cancelled. There was only a single operational sortie when F/Lt. Ross took off in Hurricane Z3763 at 17.55 to "investigate noise above clouds", landing at 18.25, having failed to locate the aircraft.

There were a number of practice flights by 134 Squadron; BD699 (Sgt. Clarke) and Z5123 (Sgt. Kirvan), taking off at 09.45 hours for formation flying practice; landing at 10.45. At 17.40 hours two Hurricanes, Z5236 (P/O. Elkington) and BD 790 (Sgt. Fry), took off for local flying practice, joined by Hurricane Z5159 (P/O. Wollaston), which took off at 17.50, all three landing at 18.20.

Training flights with Soviet Pilots continued using Z4012. Captain Savanov took off at 16.00, conducting gun firing practice into a local lake, landing at 16.20; Captain Kuharenko then took the aircraft up and conducted gun firing practice into the lake, landing at 17.00.

3.10.1941: There was no operational flying by 134 Squadron; the only sorties being two weather test flights. Hurricane Z5205 (S/Ldr. Miller), took off at 08.05, landing at 08.20. Z3978 (P/O. Cameron) took off at 15.00 and landed at 15.15.

4.10.1941: Weather again precluded any operational flying. Only a single weather test sortie was flown; Z5236 (P/O. Elkington) taking off at 09.30, landing at 09.50.

5.10.1941: No flying. Weather cold, snow and sleet in the afternoon.

6.10.1941: There was no operational flying in the morning. Local flying practice was conducted using Hurricane Z5208 by three Soviet pilots. Captains Savanov, Policovnicov and Pogarielli, each flying in turn between 10.15 and 11.55 hours.

'A' Flight launched six Hurricanes, Z3978 (P/O. Cameron), Z5134 (Sgt. Gould), Z5303 (Sgt Campbell), Z5253 (P/O. Furneaux), BD699 (Sgt. Kirvan) and Z5311 (Sgt. Kiel), which took off on patrol at 15.30. This Flight is also recorded in some documentation as being practice flights. Regardless, while the aircraft were airborne information was received about a formation of German Ju.88 bombers heading towards the Murmansk/Vayenga area.

The details of the ensuing action are outlined in the No. 134 Squadron narrative here reproduced verbatim:

"6 aircraft "A" Flight 134 Squadron (3. 12 M.G. & 3. 10 M.G.) took off from Vayenga at 15.30 hrs. for practice flying. After 35 minutes when over the aerodrome at 3000 feet, were ordered to patrol between zone 2 and 5 at 3000 ft. Then told to patrol zone 3 as enemy bombers were approaching Murmansk. When climbing to 4000 ft in centre of zone 3 Red 1 saw smoke trails at 11,000 ft towards Vyaenga. There also appeared

to be about 20 E.A. approaching Murmansk from the East at 10,000 ft above the cloud. These were not attacked. (Cloud 6/10 at 10.000 ft) A.A. then opened up. Smoke trails stopped as E.A. started diving and flight lost sight of E.A.

"A" Flight turned N. and saw 2 or 3 E.A. diving on the aerodrome from the S.W. Red 1 ordered "A" Flight N.E. to head off the E.A. "A" flight at 8,000 ft in pairs line astern intercepted a ragged formation JU.88's heading East at same height. A dog-fight ensued.

Red I P/O Cameron (12 M.G.) attacked the leader of the JU.88's firing a 5 second burst from slightly below and on the stern quarter, opening at 300 yds closing to 100 yds. No return fire. Starboard engine of E.A. emitted a stream of black smoke. This aircraft is claimed as damaged. Red 1 broke away and attacked the second A.C. in the formation also from quarter astern opening at 250 yds, and closing to 50 yds., no results were seen. Red 1 broke away and attacked a third JU.88 from head on, passing underneath E.A. turned to port and saw that E.A. was going slowly at a steep angle, it appeared that both engines had been hit. Two Hurricanes approaching from the South under the E.A. turned to port and were last seen about to attack the E.A. This E.A. is claimed as probable and may have been destroyed by the other Hurricanes.

Red 2 P/O Furneaux dived to a JU88 and attacked from above and astern firing a second burst from 200 yards without visible results. Red 2 then delivered a series of quarter astern attacks from alternate sides. After the second attack the port engine caught fire and pieces fell off striking Red 2's mainplane and tail plane. Another Hurricane, S/Ldr. Rook (81 Squadron), joined these attacks. During a subsequent attack a large piece from the starboard engine fell off. The starboard engine eventually caught fire and the aircraft was seen to crash.

Sgt Gould, Yellow 1 (10 M.G's) was top weaver and mistaking 81 Squadron for E.A. took evasive action in a steep turn losing height. He then turned East and climbed. When at 4000 ft he saw a JU.88 diving towards him and fired a burst head on from 600 yds closing until he had to break away over the E.A. He saw his bullets strike between the port engine and the fuselage and pieces of the E.A. fall off. He did not see the E.A. again. This JU.88 is claimed as damaged.

Sgt Kirvan, Yellow 2 (12 M.G's) was bottom weaver, and did a steep turn to port to avoid 81 Squadron. He was facing West at 8000 ft when he saw a JU.88 diving towards the West behind him. He throttled back and fired a short burst 1 ring deflection from about 500 yards. Yellow 2 then got on to E.A. tail and fired 4 bursts from dead astern at 200 yds but observed no effect. Return fire from E.A. He then made 2 astern attacks from 250 yds but saw no effects. He then saw another Hurricane (81 Sqdn) who continued the attack.

Yellow 2 broke away as E.A. was flying over an aerodrome near the front line, and a few moments later saw a small fire on the JU.88 which was at about 500 ft.

White 1 Sgt Campbell (10 M.G.'s) and White 2 Sgt Keil (10 M.G.'s) both did steep turns to port on seeing JU.88's followed by aircraft which turned out to be 81 Sqdn, and were unable to engage.

3 Aircraft "B" Flight took off at 16.10 hrs when the aerodrome was being bombed and turned West gaining height. The remainder of "B" Flight took off but were too late to engage the E.A. They saw A.A. fire from the river. Green 1 F/O Elkington climbed to 8000 ft onto the tail of the JU.88, firing two long bursts and saw his bullets strike the tail of the E.A. The tail unit was flapping and E.A. started diving. Black 1 F/Sgt Barnes then closed in and fired long bursts from above and astern opening at 150 yds and closing to 50 yds. Black smoke poured from the starboard engine, E.A. was almost at ground level and slowed up and swayed to starboard. Return fire in twin streams was observed. This ceased after F/Sgt Barnes' third attack. Black 1 climbed and fired a fifth burst from the port quarter from 100 yards. This aircraft is claimed as probable, and was seen by F/Sgt McCann to be well alight.

Squadron landed at 16.40 hours.

The JU.88's had black crosses with yellow edges, and orange on the undersurface of the wing tips. 134 Squadron had no difficulty in catching up with the JU.88's.

Our casualties:	Nil	
Enemy Casualties:	P/O Furneaux)	
	S/Ldr Rook.)	1 JU.88. Destroyed
	P/O Cameron..	1 JU.88 probable
		1 JU.88 Damaged
	Sgt. Gould.	1 JU.88 Damaged
	F/O Elkington)	
	F/Sgt. Barnes)	1 JU.88 Destroyed.

'B' Flight aircraft, pilots and scramble time:

Z5159 (P/O. Wollaston, Z5236 (P/O. Elkington), Z5120 (F/Sgt. Barnes) and Z5226 (F/Sgt. McCann) scrambled and took off at 16.10. BD790 (Sgt. Griffiths) and Z5205 (S/Ldr. Miller) took off at 16.15. All 'B' Flight aircraft landed between 16.25 and 16.50.

REPORT ON AIR RAID AT VYAENGA
Aerodrome on October 6th, 1941.

Attack commenced approx. 16.10 hours. (Handwritten)

In the course of the raid approx. 20 bombs are believed to have been dropped on the aerodrome in immediate vicinity. Calibre mainly 50 or 100 kilos with several 250 or 300 kilos.

The first bombs dropped on Western side of drome near dispersal point of 81 Squadron some dropped in a line across landing ground and remainder on Eastern side, near or in the lake.

One bomb exploded near Wing Engineer Officers' (F/L V.A. Gittins) dugout on East side, and blast lifted him and three airmen off ground in entrance to dugout and blew them inside, causing slight abrasions to F/L Gittins knees. 3 or 4 more bombs exploded in same vicinity shortly afterwards.

One airman (81 Squadron) sustained leg injury by bomb fragment whilst crossing field; F/L V.A. Gittins rendered first aid and conveyed airman to sick bay.

Two M/T. vehicles were struck by bomb fragments and rendered U/S for 2 hours.

4 bombs (approx 100 kilos) dropped in confined area on East side of drome apparently having been jettisoned. One exploded, remainder did not explode apparently being faulty and subsequently detonated by Soviet authorities.

One JU.88 dived (illegible hand writing has replaced 'and machine gunned') flying field and 2 Hurricanes of 81 Squadron attempting to take off.

A No.134 Squadron Hurricane IIB, removed from its 'hide', is serviced at wintry Vayenga, guarded by a Soviet sentry. RAF

7.10.1941: After the drama of the previous day, there were only two operational sorties on the 7th. At 08.30 two Hurricanes, Z5205 (S/Ldr. Miller) and BD699 (Sgt. Clarke) took off on patrol to "investigate a noise above the cloud", landing at 09.20.

Two Hurricanes, Z3765 (F/Lt. Ross) and Z5120 (F/Sgt. Barnes) took off on weather test flights at 16.20 hours, landing at 16.50 hours.

There was one local practice flight by a Soviet Pilot, Captain Pogarelli taking off in Z5208 at 11.10, landing at 11.40.

8.10.1941: At 11.40, 'B' Flight launched six Hurricanes, Z3763 (F/Lt. Ross), Z5120 (Sgt. Fry), Z5236 (P/O. Elkington), BD790 (Sgt. Douglas), Z5226 (F/Sgt. McCann) and Z5159 (P/O Wollaston). This was followed by the launch of six 'A' Flight Hurricanes, Z5205 (S/Ldr. Miller), Z5125 (Sgt. Kirvan), Z3978 (P/O. Cameron), Z5303 (Sgt. Gould), BD699 (Sgt. Clarke) and Z5211 (Sgt. Kiel), at 11.45. 'B' Flight was to provide close escort to 7 Soviet "SB" bombers;

The bombers at 8,000 ft, with 'B' Flight Hurricanes at 14,000 ft. 'A' Flight were to fly top cover at 17,000 ft. The bombers dropped their bombs on the target area, which was located "at Northern end of front line". However, 6/10th cloud cover at 3-5,000 ft meant 134 Squadron could not report on effects.

'B' Flight landed at 13.10, 'A' Flight landing at various times between 12.10 and 13.25. Once refueled, five of the 'B' Flight aircraft, Z3763 (F/Lt. Ross), Z5236 (P/O. Elkington), Z5226 (F/Sgt. McCann), Z5120 (Sgt. Fry) and BD790 (Sgt. Douglas), took off again at 13.25 (BD790 took off at 13.30) to intercept enemy bombers in Zone 2. No enemy aircraft were encountered and the Flight was ordered to patrol Zone 4, returning to base and landing at 14.50.

Six Hurricanes of 'A' Flight and 2 of 'B' Flight, Z5205 (S/Ldr. Miller), Z5123 (Sgt. Kirvan), Z5253 (P/O. Furneaux), Z5303 (Sgt. Gould), BD699 (Sgt. Clarke), Z5211 (Sgt. Kiel), Z5159 (P/O. Wollaston) and Z5120 (Sgt. Fry), took off at 14.40 hours to patrol Zone 2 to intercept German bombers reported in the area. P/O. Wollaston and Sgt. Fry were detached to patrol Zone 4. All eight Hurricanes landed between 15.25 and 15.30.

Training flights with Soviet pilots continued; six flights being conducted under the supervision of F/Lt. Ross, known to the Soviet pilots as 'Capitan'. The Soviet pilots' Capt's Kuharenko, Pogarelli, Polcovnicov, Rodin and Algorov, flew Hurricane Z4017 in turn between 11.30 hours and 14.20 hours.

9-10.10.1941: There was no operational flying on these dates; weather being generally squally with outbreaks of snow and sleet. On the 10th, P/O. Sheldon took Hurricane Z5211 up on a weather test at 12.00, landing at 12.20. Soviet pilots continued practice flights; five flights in all being conducted between 12.00 and 13.45 using Hurricanes Z4017 and Z5208. Flights consisted of Z4017 (Cap. Savonov) and Z5208 (Cap. Kukarenko), take offs 12.00 and landings 12.30 and 12.35 respectively. Z5208 (Cap. Polcovnicov), take off 12.50, landing 13.15, Z4017 (Cap. Pogarelli), take off 12.45, landing 13.00 and Z5208 (Leut. Rodin), take off 13.20, landing 13.45.

11.10.1941: Again there was no operational flying due to weather. Snow showers had accumulated to 12 inches lying in some areas. There were three Soviet pilot flights. Z5208 (Cap. Savonov) took off at 09.40 on a weather test flight, at 10.00. Z5208 (Cap. Savonov) and Z4017 (Cap. Polcovnicov) took off on practice flights at 12.45, landing at 13.15.

12.10.1941: The deep snow of the previous few days had been rolled in on the take-off and landing field, which then froze in, providing a good operating surface.

At 16.00 hours 'B' Flight launched six Hurricanes, Z3763 (F/Lt. Ross), BD790 (Sgt. Griffiths), Z5226 (F/Sgt. McCann), Z5120 (Sgt. Knapton), Z5236 (P/O. Elkington) and Z5159 (P/O. Wollaston); Flight to patrol Zone 1 at

12,000 ft following a report that 4 Me.110's were operating West of Murmansk. Visibility was estimated at 50 miles, but no enemy aircraft were encountered. 'B' Flight landed at 16.55 with the exception of P/O. Wollaston, who landed at 17.00.

Soviet pilots continued Hurricane practice flights; ten sorties being conducted by ten pilots, each flying a single sortie between 10.40 and 14.00. Total flying tome for the Soviet pilots was 6 hours and ten minutes with two Hurricanes, Z4017 and Z5208.

13.10.1941: No. 134 Squadron was tasked with one operation; escorting Soviet bombers, which were to bomb a target area some 13 miles from Petsamo. However, low cloud which rolled in during the afternoon led to this operation being cancelled.

Hurricanes Z4017 and Z5208 were used on 11 practice flights by ten Soviet pilots; one pilot flying twice. These flights were conducted between 10.05 and 14.00 hours.

14.10.1941: There was no Hurricane flying due to heavy mist. A new batch of Soviet pilots had arrived for Hurricane conversion and these were taken on a ground instructional tour of the aircraft at dispersal.

15.10.1941: There were reports that 4 enemy Ju.88 bombers had left their base at Banak, Norway. These aircraft were expected to be over the No.134 Squadron Sector at 16.00 hours. Six pilots from 'B' Flight were put on standby at 15.45, but were stood down at 16.10. However, within 2 minutes of being told "the flap was over", it was reported that Murmansk (12 miles away) was being bombed. The six 'B' Flight Hurricanes, Z3763 (F/Lt. Ross), Z5120 (Sgt. Fry), Z5236 (P/O. Elkington), BD790 (Sgt. Douglas), Z5226 (F/Sgt. McCann) and Z5159 (P/O. Wollaston), took off on base patrol at 16.35. Five 'A' Flight Hurricanes, Z5205 (S/Ldr. Miller), Z5134 (Sgt. Gould), Z3978 (P/O. Cameron), Z5123 (Sgt. Clarke) and Z5211 (Sgt. Kirvan) took off at 16.40, but all Squadron aircraft were too late to intercept the German bombers and returned to base; all 11 Hurricanes landing between 16.55 and 17.05.

Soviet pilots continued Hurricane training flights with no less than 14 sorties flown by 14 pilots; this including 1 weather test flight, between 10.05 and 14.30.

16.10.1941: Eleven Hurricanes, Z5205 (S/Ldr. Miller), Z5303 (Sgt. Campbell), Z3978 (P/O. Cameron), Z5134 (Sgt. Kiel), Z5253 (P/O. Furneaux), Z5123 (P/O. Sheldon), Z3763 (F/Lt. Ross), Z5120 (Sgt. Fry), Z5236 (P/O. Elkington), Z5159 (Sgt. Knapton) and BD790 (Sgt. Griffiths), took off at 13.15 to escort nine Soviet bombers, 6 SB.2's and 3 SB.3's. 'A' Flight was close escort at 12,000 ft, while 'B' Flight was top cover at 14.000 ft. The Soviet bombers dropped their bombs "on inlet at Northern end of front". Only a single burst of anti aircraft was noticed by the Squadron and no enemy aircraft were encountered. The Squadrons Hurricanes landed between 14.10 and 14.20.

At 15.35 Soviet pilot Cap. Savonov was scrambled in Hurricane Z4012, followed by three 134 Squadron Hurricanes with 134 Squadron pilots; Z5236 (P/O. Elkington), Z5120 (Sgt. Douglas) and Z5159 (Sgt. Knapton). Six more Hurricanes were scrambled at 15.45; Z5205 (S/Ldr. Miller), Z5303 (Sgt. Campbell), Z3978 (P/O. Cameron), Z5134 (Sgt. Kiel), Z5252 (P/O. Furneaux) and Z5123 (P/O. Sheldon). One other Hurricane, Z3763 (F/Lt. Ross), is noted as having scrambled at 15.55. The Hurricanes were tasked with intercepting Ju.88's that were attacking the aerodrome, but were too late to intercept. The aerodrome was bombed; "about 7 bombs were dropped in area of drome, 2 on hills on West side, 3 on flying field approx. ¾ mile from Northern end, 2 in or on edge of lake on East side. No damage or casualties".

The Soviet pilot took off five minutes before any No.134 Squadron pilots. The Form 540 states "10 aircraft took off to intercept 3 JU.88's attacking aerodrome but too late to intercept. Soviet pilots took off considerable time earlier, having apparently received prior information".

Between 08.35 and 13.40 hours, 13 practice sorties were flown by Soviet pilots in 10 hours, 29 minutes flying time on Hurricanes Z4012, Z5208, Z5122 and Z4017.

17.10.1941: No.134 Squadron was tasked to escort Soviet bombers attacking 'Hill 389' in the battle front. Twelve Hurricanes, Z3978 (P/O. Cameron), Z5205 (Sgt. Kiel), Z5253 (P/O. Furneaux), Z5134 (Sgt. Gould), Z5123 (P/O. Sheldon), Z5303 (Sgt. Clarke), Z3763 (F/Lt. Ross), Z5226 (F/Sgt. McCann), Z5159 (Sgt. Knapton), Z5120 (Sgt. Douglas), Z5236 (Sgt. Griffiths) and BD790 (Sgt. Fry), took off at 09.30. P/O. Cameron, 'A' Flight leader, was forced to return and land at 09.40 due to magnetic trouble. The remaining 11 Hurricanes escorted 6 SB.2 and 2 SB.3 bombers, which bombed the target area, the effects of which were not observed by 134 Squadron pilots. No enemy aircraft were encountered and the Squadron landed between 10.45 and 11.00 hours.

There were two air raids in the district of the aerodrome in the afternoon, but although there was anti aircraft fire, no bombs were dropped on or near the aerodrome.

At 13.55 hours ten 134 Squadron Hurricanes were scrambled with pilots from 81 Squadron, Z5205 (S/Ldr. Rook), Z5253 (P/O. Walker), Z3978 (F/O. McGregor), Z5123 (Sgt. Sims), Z5134 (F/Sgt. Haw), Z5303 (Sgt. Waud), Z5226 (Sgt. Crewe), Z3763 (P/O. Holmes), Z5120 (P/O. Bush) and BD790 (Sgt. Reed). No enemy aircraft were encountered and the Hurricanes returned, landing between 14.25 and 14.45.

At 15.55 there was another scramble, again 81 Squadron pilots flying 134 Squadron Hurricanes, Z5205 (S/Ldr. Rook), Z5253 (P/O. Walker), Z3978 (P/O. McGregor), Z5123 (Sgt. Sims), Z5134 (F/Sgt. Haw) and Z5303 (Sgt.

Waud). Again no enemy aircraft were encountered and the Hurricanes returned to land between 16.40 and 16.45.

Soviet practice flying in Hurricanes increased with 18 sorties flown in 11 hours, 40 minutes flying time between 08.25 and 14.45. Three Hurricanes, Z4017, Z5122 and Z5208, were used for the Soviet training flights.

18.10.1941: P/O. Cameron conducted a weather test flight in Z3968, taking off at 09.35 and landing at 09.50. 'A' Flight was at readiness during the morning, being scrambled, at 10.00 hours. Six Hurricanes, Z3968 (P/O. Cameron), Z5211 (Sgt. Kiel), Z5123 (P/O. Sheldon), Z5205 (Sgt. Gould), Z5253 (Sgt. Clarke) and Z5303 (Sgt. Campbell, attempted to intercept two Focke Wulf 200 Condor four engine aircraft in Zone 2, but did not see the enemy aircraft and returned to base, landing between 10.45 and 10.50 hours.

At 12.20 hours, 3 No.134 Squadron Hurricanes with Soviet pilots, Z5236 (Lt. Kravchinko), Z5226 (Lt. Verchooski) and Z4012 (Lt. Rodin), were scrambled for aerodrome defence; two landing at 13.00 and the other at 13.20.

Six 'A' Flight Hurricanes, Z3978 (P/O. Cameron), Z5211 (Sgt. Kiel), Z5123 (P/O. Sheldon), Z5205 (Sgt. Gould), Z5253 (Sgt. Clarke) and Z5303 (Sgt. Campbell), were scrambled at 12.25, landing a 13.20.

Two 134 Squadron Hurricanes with Soviet pilots, Z5226 (Cap. Reutov) and BD790 (Cap. Sinev), were scrambled at 14.15, landing at 15.00.

Six 'B' Flight Hurricanes, Z5205 (S/Ldr. Miller), Z5211 (Sgt. Fry), Z5213 (P/O. Elkington), Z3978 (Sgt. Griffiths), Z5253 (Sgt. Knapton) and Z5303 (Sgt. Douglas), were scrambled for a base patrol at 15.45, landing between 16.40 and 16.45.

Two 134 Squadron Hurricanes with Soviet pilots, Z5226 (Cap. Algorov) and BD790 (Cap. Hrustal, were scrambled for a base patrol at 16.10, landing at 17.00.

Six 'B' Flight Hurricanes, Z5205 (S/Ldr. Miller), Z5211 (Sgt. Fry), Z5123 (P/O. Elkington), Z3978 (Sgt. Griffiths), Z5253 (Sgt. Knapton) and Z5303 (Sgt. Douglas), were scrambled for a base patrol at 17.10, landing at 17.50. These were the last operational sorties of any of the 151 Wing Hurricane Squadron in North Russia. The last 134 Squadron sortie of the day, however, was a non-operational air test flown by Sgt. Clarke in BD699; take off at 17.45 and landing at 18.00.

During this last day of operations of No.134 Squadron, 'B' Flight used some 'A' Flight aircraft for their patrols. It should be noted that while it is noted above that Soviet pilots were flying operations on this date with 134 Squadron aircraft, this is because they are recorded in 134 Squadrons operational records as such. However, these sorties were actually the commencment of operations by the Soviet Hurricane Squadrons.

As the early evening sunlight fades over Vayenga aerodrome ground crew service a No.134 Squadron Hurricane IIB mounted on trestles. RAF

On the 19th, 134 Squadron handed its Hurricanes over to the Soviets, although ground crew continued to "supervise Soviet operations". On the 15th, the Hurricanes of 'A' Flight No.81 Squadrons were handed over to the Soviets; Soviet pilots flying 6 sorties in them that day. On the 22nd, 81 Squadron handed its remaining Hurricanes to the Soviets, although some Squadron personnel continued supervisory operations with the Soviet No.1 Hurricane Squadron.

On 22 October, "Headquarters, 151 Wing, assumed complete administrative control of 81 and 134 Squadron,. Adjutants instructed to place themselves at disposal of Wing Adjutant to assist in administrative duties". To all intents and purposes No.81 and 134 Squadrons ceased to exist as independent units form this date; the personnel returning to the United Kingdom in November 1941.

POSTSCRIPT

INITIAL OPERATIONS NO.1 SOVIET HURRICANE SQUADRON OCTOBER 1941

On the 15th, Soviet Air Force pilots took possession of the Hurricanes of 'A' Flight No.81 Squadron RAF, flying six sorties in them that day, totaling 3 hours and 15 minutes flying time. On the 19th October, the No.134 Squadron Hurricanes were officially handed over to the Soviet Union for operations with No.1 Soviet Hurricane Squadron. On the 22nd, the remaining 81 Squadron Hurricanes were taken over by the Soviet Air Force

On inheriting the former No.81 and 134 Squadron Hurricanes, the Soviet's organised these into operational units. "Squadron is composed of 12 machines in sections of 3. Each machine has ground crew of 2 Flight Mechanics, and each section of 3 planes is supervised by an N.C.O. Flight Mechanic. Initially two only 'Wireless Mechanics' have been supplied for wireless equipment duties in the Squadron, and only one 'Electrician' for duties in three Squadrons of 12 machines each. The inadequate personnel has been pointed out by Wing Specialist Officers".

On 26 October 1941, the new Soviet Hurricane Squadron claimed its first enemy aircraft destroyed when a former 134 Squadron Hurricane was used to shoot down an enemy Me.110 fighter. One of the Hurricanes returned from this combat with damage inflicted by enemy cannon shells. At this time, No.134 Squadron ground crew was still supervising ground operations of the Soviet Hurricane Squadron.

APPENDICES

Appendix I

Hawker Hurricane

The Hawker Hurricane was designed as a single seat, low wing cantilever monoplane, featuring retractable undercarriage, and partial span split flaps. The aircraft prototype flew in 1936 and the first operational variant, the Hurricane MK. I entered service with No.111 Squadron RAF in December 1937. The aircraft was the mainstay of RAF Fighter Command and the British Air Forces in France during battles in May and June 1940; one Squadron also operating in Norway. Following the evacuation of Norway and the fall of France, Fighter Command, consisted mainly of Hurricanes and Spitfires, countered the Luftwaffe; leading to the Battle of Britain during the summer and autumn months.

The MK II Hurricane's main difference over the MK I was the installation of a Merlin XX engine instead of the Merlin III of the earlier variant. There were other differences, but initially the eight 0.303 in machine gun armament of the MK I was retained in the MK. II, this being the MK.IIA. The MK.IIB introduced the new wing with a 12 gun armament; adding four additional machine guns in the outer wings.

The MK II Hurricane had a maximum speed in the order of 340 MPH at optimum altitude, which was around 15 miles or so slower than the Me.109E. That said, different tests showed different maximum speeds for the 109E, ranging from 342 to 354 MPH.

Me.109E

The standard fighter of the Luftwaffe during the hectic air battles of 1940, the Me.109E was still in widespread operational service with the Luftwaffe in late 1941. A low wing monoplane, the aircraft was superior in some respects to the Hurricane and inferior in others. Armament was a mixture of machine guns and cannon

The following comes from the conclusion of a document on comparative trials between the Me.109 and a Hurricane conducted in May 1940. Although this trial involved a Hurricane MK.I, the conclusions remain relative; although the speed margin the Me.109 had over the Hurricane I was reduced in the Hurricane MK .II.

"The M.E.109 is faster than the Hurricane by some 30 to 40 miles an hour on the straight and level. It can out-climb and initially out-dive the Hurricane. On the other hand it has not the maneuverability of the Hurricane, which can turn inside without difficulty. After this clear-cut demonstration of superior maneuverability there is no doubt in my mind that provided Hurricanes are not surprised by 109's, that the odds are not more than two to one, and the pilots use their heads, the balance will always be in favour of our aircraft, one the 109's have committed themselves to combat."

During its operational existence in North Russia the two Squadrons of No.151 Wing were equipped with the Hawker Hurricane MK IIB, which differed from the Hurricane IIA (top and above) in that it could be armed with 12 x 0.303 inch guns, whereas the IIA was armed with eight guns. The Hurricane IIB's deployed to Russia in September 1941 were equipped with tropical filters. USAF

The Me.109 (top) and the Ju.88 (above) were the two types most encountered by
No.151 Wing Hurricanes in Russia. Featured are the Me.109G and a Ju.88D. The
Hurricanes of 151 Wing encountered Me.109E and F models. USAF

Hurricane II

Engine		Rolls Royce Merlin XX
Ratings	Take off	1300 hp at 3000 rpm
	Normal	1255 hp at 2850 rpm at 10,000 ft
	Maximum	1270 hp at 3000 rpm at 12,500 ft (low blower)
	Maximum	1185 hp at 3000 rpm at 21,000 ft (high blower)
Gear ratio		0.477:1
Propeller		Rotol constant speed (wood blades)
Diameter		11 ft 4 in
Number of blades		3
Fuel capacity		94 Imperial gal
Oil capacity		7.5 Imperial gal
Wright (empty)		5486 lb
Normal gross weight		6854 lb
Wing loading (normal gross weight)		26.6 lb/sq ft
Power loading (normal gross weight		5.45 lb/hp
Overall height (datum line level)		12 ft 2 in
Overall length		31 ft 6 in
Wing span		40 ft
Wing area		257.6 sq ft
Aspect ratio		6.22
Taper ratio		2.03:1
Dihedral (outer panels)		+3.5 degrees
Incidence (with fuselage datum)		+2.0 degrees - +/- 0.5 a degree
Wing flaps (split T.E type) area		25.11 sq ft
Wing flap (semi-span)		9 ft 6 in
Aileron length (each)		7 ft 8.5 in
Aileron area (total area, each)		10.2 sq ft
Stabaliser (fixed)		
Maxim chord		2 ft 8 in
Area (including 2.5 sq ft fuselage)		24.1 sq ft
Elevator		
Span		11 ft 0 in
Maximum chord		1 ft 6.5 in
Vertical fin		
Area		8.3 sq ft
Rudder		
Vertical		6 ft 5 and a quarter

Appendix II

No.81 Squadron Aircraft deployed to North Russia

BD697
BD792
BD818
BD822
Z3746
Z3768
Z3977
Z4006
Z4017
Z4018
Z5107
Z5122
Z5157
Z5207
Z5208
Z5209
Z5227
Z5122
Z5228

No.134 Squadron Aircraft deployed to North Russia

BD699
BD790
BD825
Z3978
Z3763
Z3978
Z4012
Z4013
Z5120
Z5123
Z5134
Z5159
Z5205
Z5206
Z5210
Z5211
Z5226
Z5236
Z5253
Z5303
Z5763

GLOSSARY

Adjt.	Adjutant
AFC	Air Force Cross
CO	Commanding Officer
Discip.	Discipline
F/O	Flying Officer
F/Lt	Flight Lieutenant
F/Sgt	Flight Sergeant
HMS	His Majesty's Ship
JU.	Junkers
ME.	Messerschmitt
NCO	Non Commissioned Officer
No.	Number
P/O	Pilot Officer
RAF	Royal Air Force
Sgt.	Sergeant
S/Ldr	Squadron Leader

BIBLIOGRAPHY

No.81 Squadron Operation Record Book Summary of Events 1 July – 30 September 1941

No.81 Squadron Operation Record Book Record of Events 1 July – 30 September 1941

No.81 Squadron Operation Record Book Record of Events 1 – 31 October 1941

No.134 Squadron Operation Record Book Summary of Events 1 July – 30 September 1941

No.134 Squadron Operation Record Book Record of Events 1 July – 30 September 1941

No.134 Squadron Operation Record Book Record of Events 1 – 31 October 1941

No.81 Squadron Combat Reports for September and October 1941

No.134 Squadron Combat Reports for October 1941

Composite interview with 81 and 134 Squadron personnel (Translated from Russian language)

No. 81 Squadron Narrative of Operations on 6 October 1941

No. 134 Squadron Narrative of Operations on 6 October 1941

No.151 Wing Headquarters and No.81 and No.134 Squadron Movement Order for August 1941

Headquarters Fighter Command Movement Order, Signal 0.89 Dated 27/7/41

No.151 Wing Report On Air Raid at Vyaenga Aerodrome on October 6th, 1941

Soviet 'Red Planet' article (English translation)

Report of Comparative Trials of Hurricane versus Messerschmitt 109, dated 7 May 1940

Report on Flying Qualities of the Hurricane MK II

In addition several hundred pages of miscellaneous pages of documents; operational and command and political were consulted.

Note: For the most part aerodrome from which 151 Wing operated in Russia has been referred to as Vayenga. However, this aerodrome has been referred to in various documents and translations as Vayenga, Vayaenga Vyaenga, Vaenga among others.

6542029R00041

Printed in Great Britain
by Amazon.co.uk, Ltd.,
Marston Gate.